RESEARCH, WRITE, CREATE

Connecting Scholarship and Digital Media

Twyla Gibson
Mark Lipton

OXFORD
UNIVERSITY PRESS

OXFORD
UNIVERSITY PRESS

Oxford University Press is a department of the University of Oxford.
It furthers the University's objective of excellence in research, scholarship,
and education by publishing worldwide. Oxford is a registered trade mark of
Oxford University Press in the UK and in certain other countries.

Published in Canada by
Oxford University Press
8 Sampson Mews, Suite 204,
Don Mills, Ontario M3C 0H5 Canada

www.oupcanada.com

Library and Archives Canada Cataloguing in Publication

Gibson, Twyla, 1954–, author
Research, write, create : connecting scholarship and digital media
/ Twyla Gibson and Mark Lipton.

Includes bibliographical references and index.
ISBN 978-0-19-544741-5 (pbk.)

1. Report writing. 2. Research. 3. Report writing—Computer network
resources. 4. Research—Computer network resources. 5. Digital media.
6. Learning and scholarship. I. Lipton, Mark, author II. Title.

LB2369.G55 2013   808.02   C2013-902928-1

Cover image: diane555/iStockphoto

Photo credits: Page 48 © Vecdog/istockphoto; page 59 created at www.wordle.net;
page 69 © Antonio/istockphoto; page 186 George Grall/National Geographic Creative.

Oxford University Press is committed to our environment.
This book is printed on Forest Stewardship Council® certified paper
and comes from responsible sources.

Printed and bound in Canada

1 2 3 4 — 17 16 15 14

Contents

13 · Analysis, Results, and Conclusion

Author Biographies

Twyla Gibson is an assistant professor at the iSchool (Information Science & Learning Technologies) at the University of Missouri, where she teaches courses on digital humanities, history and philosophy of information and media, academic libraries, and visual communication and culture. She also holds an appointment as assistant professor of culture and technology at the Faculty of Information at the University of Toronto. She is a founding editor of the peer-reviewed journal *MediaTropes* and has published widely on revolutionary shifts in communication and information media and technologies. Her research on digital technologies for the analysis of ancient texts is supported by the Social Science and Humanities Research Council of Canada.

Mark Lipton is associate professor in the School of English and Theatre Studies at the University of Guelph, where he is cross-appointed to the Media Studies program at Guelph–Humber. He teaches courses on media, communication, digital literacy and pedagogy, performance studies, and research methods and publishes in these and other areas. In 2009, as a result of his work with the *Media Education Project*, he was awarded the Jacque Ellul Award for Outstanding Media Ecology Activism.

Preface

Introduction

Welcome to scholarly research in the age of new technology! Advances in information and communication media are altering institutions, the economy, society, and culture as well as changing the way we learn, work, play, and relate. Universities, archives, libraries, and museums are reorganizing and retooling to remain relevant to the needs of users in a highly technological society. Academic labour is being redefined as computer enabled research is incorporated into scholarly traditions. Even staid humanities disciplines are in transition as computationally intensive research techniques are combined with traditional methods.

Today, students can experiment with tools, techniques, and approaches on the leading edge of technological developments in academic research. Innovative methods and devices build on traditional approaches and provide new ways to address long-standing questions, theories, and methods. Ultimately, using new technologies for academic research raises questions and suggests avenues for scholarship that were not open using traditional means. Rarely have there been more opportunities for student researchers to make their mark on scholarship.

The Digital Essay

Digital essay is the term we use when talking about scholarly work that incorporates digital media and methods in an integrative framework. A conventional research essay is typically a text printed in black ink on white paper. Most often, it is meant to be read in linear fashion from beginning to end. By contrast, a digital essay is a multimodal interactive document that includes images, sounds, music, video, links, colour, and other enhancements to the text.

Whereas a traditional paper is a physical document that must be distributed by hand, the digital essay is an electronic document that can be posted online and accessed by anyone with an Internet connection. In addition, the digital essay can be presented using PowerPoint, Prezi, or Keynote. Minus such enhancements as music and links, it can be printed and presented as a conventional text document. The digital essay, then, includes all the features that characterize the traditional text-based essay—and more.

The printed paper is a traditional intellectual product that evolved over several centuries. The digital essay is the next stage in that evolution. As a new researcher in the digital age, you have the opportunity to contribute to both the expansion of knowledge and the ongoing development of the scholarly essay.

The Book and Website

This book and the companion website have been designed to work together. The two pieces function in tandem to help you improve your efficiency and effectiveness, to keep you up to date on the most recent digital tools and techniques, and to guide you smoothly through the steps involved in bringing the different aspects of your research together to produce a compelling piece of work that successfully integrates digital media and scholarship.

The Book

The book provides a general explanation of the various kinds of digital tools. It describes how you can use these tools to produce a project that fulfills the criteria established by your instructor or department—and yet goes beyond what can be accomplished in a traditional paper.

The process of producing a scholarly research project is ordered into a series of organized procedures. You begin with an area of interest and gradually narrow it down to a containable topic. After investigating a range of current technologies, you engage new media to improve the effectiveness and efficiency of your research and collaborations, and you begin designing a digital product that augments your scholarly writing. Then, you craft the many components that make a solid proposal; organize a literature review into related disciplinary subfields and sections; write a critical review of the current state of knowledge; identify relevant modes of inquiry; apply appropriate methodological frameworks to analyze the data; work on producing a carefully argued analysis and interpretation of the evidence; discuss results and implications; draw conclusions; propose avenues for further research; and critically reflect on the research process.

The Website

The website provides a specific list and description of current digital resources for academic research. Since technology changes rapidly, the list will be updated regularly so you can stay up to date with existing resources, learn about new tools as they become available, and know when older media is no longer the most effective way to pursue your scholarly research. The website also has a section on key terms and a bibliography on scholarship and digital media.

◉ Be alert for this symbol—it appears throughout the book. It lets you know that you should turn to the website for more detailed information, links to tools, or examples.

Chapter Overviews

Chapter One introduces the process of researching, writing, and creating a digital essay. We discuss the relationship between academic research and the production of creative work at a post-secondary level, describe library and Internet resources, and emphasize the importance of academic integrity. We ask you to list your project ideas, create a plan for your research, and make a realistic timeline. Right from the beginning, you will want to be thinking about how to create a project that can be completed using the resources and time available to you. A checklist serves as an aid to library research.

Chapter Two helps you start conceptualizing a topic and envisioning its components. We offer advice on defining an inquiry with a narrowed focus on a specific area of research. The use of brainstorming techniques encourages you to engage in cognitive mapping exercises to further develop and elaborate a topic and project. Additionally, we ask that you begin thinking about your digital media project and the elements necessary for its design and creation. The checklist at the end of the chapter provides a list of steps for selecting and narrowing a topic.

Chapters Three, Four, and Five—while acknowledging changing digital ecologies—describe an assortment of digital tools and techniques and provide examples of the kinds of projects you might model. Many techniques are developments that combine one or more features of traditional print media. Examples help you explore underlying principles of integrating intellectual writing and digital design. In these chapters, we help you extend your digital vocabulary, develop media competency, and demonstrate fluency with today's tools and techniques.

More specifically, Chapter Three explains ways you can enhance your research through the use of blogs, microblogs, wikis for collaboration, and aggregators. Chapter Four concentrates on how social networks, podcasting, social bookmarking, and folksonomy can add depth to your scholarship. Chapter Five focuses on document sharing, VOIP technologies, digital image collections, digital and streaming video, citation managers, geotagging, geocoding, and online maps.

With background concerning digital tools and techniques as well as suggestions about how to integrate them into your project, we turn to the challenge of creating a high-caliber scholarly essay.

What makes a good proposal? This is an important question for you to consider as you begin to compose a first draft of the research you intend to conduct. Chapter Six provides a detailed formula for creating a proposal, including a basic template or format with all the elements crucial to both research and project proposals across the disciplines. These elements and their order and arrangement can be altered depending on your particular field and the parameters of your assignment. The goal of the proposal is to introduce and lay out your project, provide a review of previous research, describe the methods you will use, and explain how you will be connecting your scholarship with your digital media project. The checklist concentrates on analytic thinking and the steps involved in proposal writing.

A fundamental premise of this textbook is that the digital essay is emerging as a new genre of academic research. In order to explain what we mean by a new genre, Chapter Seven explains some of the ways that new technologies are altering scholarly production, including how scholarly documents are becoming increasingly multimodal. This chapter emphasizes research and new technologies, digital writing, the role of theories and methods, and the importance of using the academic literature to build a theoretical framework. This chapter also offers advice on understanding an assignment and distinguishing modelling from plagiarism. At the end of the chapter, there is a checklist for research protocols and meeting expectations for your assignment.

Chapter Eight describes and explains the features that characterize the major types of writing typical of scholarly work. You are given direction for writing abstracts that gain acceptance to scholarly meetings and conferences and which stand at the beginning of many academic essays, articles, and book chapters. We explain the differences between a term paper, thesis, and capstone project and suggest strategies for integrating digital media into each of these scholarly genres. We also give directions for finding appropriate associations, journals, and eResources. The checklist concentrates on conducting research and assessing literature.

Chapter Nine describes the components that need to come together in order to create an effective Introduction to your essay. This includes how to write an effective title and subtitle, and how to formulate a focused research question, hypothesis, and thesis statement. When the various parts of the Introduction are well formulated, you will have a map to guide the rest of the project. The checklist outlines the sequence of steps involved in writing the Introduction.

Chapter Ten continues the discussion of the components of the digital essay, focusing on the Review of Literature. We also discuss research paradigms (the patterns or models that govern the theories, methods, and approaches deemed acceptable in a discipline), and explain why understanding the paradigms in your field is a first step toward developing your own critique. An extended example shows how to go about incorporating digital research into your project and how to produce a critical analysis for the literature review.

Chapters Eleven and Twelve present an in-depth explanation of the Methodology section. Chapter Eleven considers the role of theories, methods, and methodologies in research. Chapter Twelve continues this discussion and explains how the Methodology section connects to other components of the study.

Chapter Thirteen outlines the key sections of the research essay that come after the Introduction, Review of Literature, and Methodology—namely the Analysis or Body of the study, the Results or Findings that emerge from the research, the Conclusion, the Bibliography, and the Appendix. This chapter describes how to draw together all the elements of your project. As you polish the various sections, you work with the total project in mind, constructing effective connections among the different parts of your study so that they all cohere in an effective unity.

Checklists in This Book

We help you apply these tools, techniques, principles, and procedures to your research by providing a checklist at the end of each chapter. Checklists will help you order tasks coherently, execute them efficiently and to a high standard, and then bring all the facets of the research into a unity to create an outstanding final project that contributes to the on-going conversation in one or more disciplines.

Let us begin.

Acknowledgements

We are grateful to Oxford University Press—Katherine Skene, Suzanne Clark, Jacqueline Mason, Phyllis Wilson, Eric Sinkins, Sherill Chapman, Lisa Ball, Peter Chambers, and especially Sarah Carmichael.

Twyla Gibson would like to thank Stuart Murray, Paul W. Gooch, Deanne Bogdan, and John Budd for their wise counsel and support. As well, she thanks Jack Silver, Laura Musselman, Marian Wihak, Giuliana and Bob Katz, and her research assistant, Daniella Levy-Pinto. In addition, she is indebted to colleagues and students at the University of Missouri, School of Information Science and Learning Technologies, colleagues and former students at the Faculty of Information and St Michael's College at the University of Toronto, and everyone at the School of English and Theatre Studies at the University of Guelph.

Mark Lipton would like to acknowledge the support of the University of Guelph, College of Arts, School of English and Theatre Studies, and the Media Studies program at the University of Guelph–Humber. He would like to thank his research assistant (and right arm) Joslyn Kilborn, and the many students and teachers who inspired this work. He also acknowledges the support of friends, family, and colleagues, especially Max Lipton and Todd McNamara.

1

Embarking on a
Research Journey

Chapter Outline

Chapter One explains the dynamics involved in researching, writing, and creating a project that integrates scholarship and new media. We explain the relationship between academic research and the production of a creative work. We also describe some of the ways that digital technologies are altering established patterns of scholarship. We present a guide to library and Internet resources—including significant library databases related to subject interests and disciplines. We also offer ways to identify preliminary search terms. As you begin your research journey, we ask that you create a tentative timeline for your project, and we stress the importance of **academic integrity**.

New Technologies and Scholarship

As computer-mediated technologies open new possibilities for intellectual work, traditional essays and theses cease to be the only kinds of documents you can produce to represent your research. **Computer archives** and **databases, social media,** and **mobile technologies** provide digital evidence that extends the traditional essay format and paves the way for new kinds of creativity.

Each new tool suggests alternative ways to approach research, different avenues for critical inquiry, and fresh venues for representing intellectual activities. New tools and techniques expand the ways that you can meet or even exceed the research goals expected of you by your professors.

These possibilities include the following:

- editing **wiki** pages;
- keeping a **blog** or **vlog** (video blog);
- tagging images in photo sharing programs;
- organizing large collections of digital content;
- producing remixes or mashups of cultural productions;
- engaging in do-it-yourself projects using low-resolution tools;
- building websites;
- producing podcasts;
- downloading, citing, tweeting, and creating collections; and
- experimenting with open access code. ◉

These are just a few examples of scholarly products that challenge the premiere position of the print paper as the only form of expression that can be submitted for academic credit (Williford and Henry 2012).

From Page to Screen

Composing an essay on a computer screen is different from writing with pen on paper. Whereas the paper page is a static black and white document, the screen is an interactive, colourful multimedia storehouse of materials that can be combined and linked in new ways.

Hyperlinked Documents

Hyperlinks in a digital essay make it possible for your reader to access the actual passage you have referenced in your footnotes, the images of a certain species of bird that you describe in detail in several paragraphs, or the maps used by air traffic controllers in your study of the most prevalent causes of airplane crashes.

Hyperlinked documents allow readers to delve more deeply into the research and to directly access the images and other sources of information you used in creating the body of evidence for your study. Hyperlinked documents do not replace traditional citation, referencing, and bibliographic requirements. You still need to follow a style guide (APA, MLA, Chicago, etc.) when quoting and pointing to the words and ideas of others. Hyperlinking is a method used in digital essays to add depth and richness to a document and to help readers follow how you have evaluated your sources for integrity, logic, and coherence.

Research and Online Publishing

Digital essays can be posted online. This means that your scholarly work can reach a much larger audience than is possible with a paper document. Wide circulation is a significant advantage. It provides opportunities for comments and feedback. It also means that your work can have real consequences. You are not just making a project because it is homework; when you put your project on the Web, you invite the world to read your arguments, hear your voice, and be influenced by your point of view. ◉⟩

Publishing online requires taking more responsibility than when producing a print document. When you post your scholarship online, you are not just a researcher, writer, and creator but also an editor, proofreader, and publisher. Irregularities, mistakes, and glitches that mar a publication will be "out there" in public. Few readers complain about one or two typos in a printed paper. However, because online publications are so public, these sorts of gaffes raise questions about the level of care that has gone into the creation of the entire project, including the research. If you plan to post your digital essay online, make sure your scholarship, editing, and proofreading are stellar so that your readers are not left with the impression that your research has been less than thorough.

Standards and Digital Scholarship

You and your professors probably share some ideas about the qualities that characterize excellence in a print document. There are few similar reference points for digital essays. Since digital research is fairly new, there are conflicting ideas and expectations about the standards that characterize high-caliber work (Williford and Henry 2012). To be safe, we suggest that you aim to produce an academic essay that meets all of the traditional criteria for scholarly research and writing in your field while,

RESEARCH IN ACTION · Jean's story

Jean's brother had joined the military and was injured while on active duty. After observing the challenges he faced when he returned home, Jean was inspired to make a short documentary about the experiences of veterans in Canada.

Jean collected war photographs and wrote a short preliminary draft of an essay that she posted on a blog. She asked readers to comment and to submit pictures, stories, or video messages that she could include in her documentary. Her request for participation circulated the globe. She discovered that veterans on all sides of conflicts had stories, images, and video footage they wanted to share.

Jean's blog turned into a primary source of material for her major research essay and digital project. She collected, organized, archived, and edited a database of veterans' stories and then selected the best material for her documentary film. To promote her documentary, she edited highlights into a **trailer** and posted it on YouTube.

at the same time, going beyond those established expectations through enhancements that include links, images, music, video, and other media.

Community and Participatory Research

Scholarship takes place within communities and it creates community. Research is about the conversation you have with other scholars, both through the ages and in dialogue with your contemporaries. The way you identify other researchers with similar interests today is through digitally mediated networks. In fact, many libraries—especially those connected with academic institutions—are moving toward models that more closely resemble nodes in a network than buildings with books. You can still walk among stacks of library books, but chances are that finding the information you seek will involve consulting an online catalogue, a series of digital databases, Google or Google Scholar, Facebook, or even Wikipedia.

Online, you can find documents and you can also take the search a step further by connecting with the authors, either through their publishers or their academic institutions here or abroad. It is fast and easy to find scholars at different institutions as well as on other continents who share similar interests, intellectual goals, and fields of specialized knowledge. Thus, new technologies offer the possibility of pursuing research and participating in intellectual communities at the local, national, and international levels in ways that were not possible for prior generations of intellectuals. Moreover, digital essays have the potential for dynamic interactions, unlike the print document's unidirectional transmission channel from one student to one professor.

Student Writing in an Era of Digital Media and Global Culture
Not long ago, when students wrote an essay, it had an intended audience of only one reader—the professor (and perhaps a teaching assistant). By contrast, the current generation of scholars finds itself creating work for a global community.

Number of Hits as Evidence of Scholarly Impact
Viewing the student essay as a community-building exercise that invites participation-intensive activities is a new phenomenon. Indeed, interaction is increasingly becoming an expectation and a key indicator of quality in a scholarly work. When others leave comments, post on your wall, retweet, or link to your work, the public attention and engagement your work has attracted is documentable evidence that your research has exceeded traditional standards and expectations for student writing. A number of online venues include tools for tracking viewers. Monitoring the number of visits to your site as well as the amount of time that is spent on each web page provides solid evidence—which you can submit to professors—that your research is having an impact.

Born-Digital Scholarship

Digital essays are beginning to appear as **born-digital** documents in peer-reviewed journals and **open-source** formats. As you conduct your research, you should be alert to professionally produced digital documents that can serve as models for your own intellectual work. In creating born-digital documents, the combination of digital media, your purposes in researching and creating, the conventions associated with the fields in which your study is embedded, and the new models of academic research that you identify online will all be factors that help you conceive, shape, and produce your study.

From Product to Ongoing Scholarly Process

Since digital essays invite an ongoing process of research, **analysis**, **synthesis**, and **multimodal** presentation compared to the more traditional finished and fixed discourses of written texts, they tend to promote a shift in emphasis from product to process. Print publications are "written in stone"—inaccuracies, omissions, or errors can only be corrected by adding **addenda** (separate sheets of paper inserted into the document that correct mistakes in the text). However, digital works can be continually revised to fix problems, upgrade content, respond to comments, add depth to the analysis, and update information as events unfold. The ability to alter a digital document when errors are recognized or when new information becomes available is another significant advantage of digital over print publications.

Changing Patterns of Research in Digital Environments

The creators of early online documents and sites have noted that digital technologies immediately led to the creation of new kinds of publications that in turn effected changes in research criteria.

From Separate Sources to Hybrid Documents

Digital media invite hybrid formations of information that in traditional publications were treated separately. Primary texts and visual images, databases of identifying information, and secondary sources "are all intermingled and easily cross-referenced. . . . Although they may have been originally created as different entities, the information they represent may be displayed as completely integrated" (Mylonas et al. 1993, 154–55). Thus your blog or digital essay can become a site of hybridity that pulls together numerous kinds of materials in an integrated presentation.

From Selective to Comprehensive Research

Digital creators also note that whereas research for paper publications must be extremely selective due to the cost of reproduction and dissemination, electronic environments call for exhaustive research. The expense of reproducing material via print publication limits the selection of information even at initial stages of data collection (e.g., colour photos were passed over in favour of black and white images that were cheaper to reproduce). By contrast, digital research produces a shift to the archival principles of collecting the "maximum amount of information possible" and storing it in "generalized form" so that it is available for future use in different formats (Mylonas et al. 1993).

From Collecting to Preserving and Curating Digital Documents

The trend to comprehensive research means that you will need to become a curator and preservationist as well as a researcher, author, editor, and publisher of information. When you take on a digital project, you must be committed to these additional roles and responsibilities that extend beyond what is required of a writer of a printed research paper.

Organizing and Indexing Digital Materials

Expanding quantities of digital material stored on your hard drive or through the use of **cloud computing** (software stored on a remote network) means that research material must be organized and indexed so you can find the information you have collected when you need it.

Updating Documents with Software Upgrades

Changing software and computing systems are additional factors you should consider when managing your scholarly materials. Ongoing introductions of more powerful computers and new and improved software programs mean that you have to monitor your materials to make sure that crucial information does not become inaccessible because it is stored on obsolete equipment or programs.

Beginning the Research Journey

These are just a few of the factors that make producing a digital document different from creating a traditional print paper and that you will need to consider when setting out on your research journey. In the next stage, you will begin using the library, evaluating the trustworthiness of sources, working with online databases, identifying keywords, and writing timelines.

The Digital Library

While many smaller libraries and archives are still organized around **brick-and-mortar models of research** that require in-person visits to access and view material, a number of larger libraries, archives, and museums have digitized their significant collections—and they are hard at work expanding the materials available on the Web. Within the next several years, many of the most important documents and artifacts held by North American and European institutions will have been digitized and made available at the click of a mouse.

Mobile Media and Wearable Computers

The growing prevalence of mobile media, the use of "apps" or **application-conditioned delivery**, and the range of wearable computer devices
(such as eyeglasses that respond to blinking or to verbal commands) on
the immediate horizon promise to radically change research done in universities, libraries, and museums. Wearable computers will revolutionize
the museum-going experience and will change the way we seek information in many different contexts. The trend to mobility suggests some possible directions that digital essays will take. One is the potential for more
information tied to geographic location. Another is the trend toward
multiple sites for delivery, customization, and reuse of scholarship. Yet
another is the increasing trend to have massive amounts of data at the tip
of your fingers no matter where you are or what time of day you need it.

Cataloguing Systems, Databases, and Peer-Reviewed Journals

University libraries pay a premium to subscribe to important databases
and peer-reviewed journals. Due to high subscription costs, these resources are not open to the public and are a significant benefit to anyone
affiliated with an academic institution. Yet too often, digital repositories
and online journals are among the resources students use least. To create
a top-tier project, you will need to hone a strategy and take full advantage
of your university's electronic resources. ◗))

Get to know your library's cataloguing system and databases, and
become fluent with the information architecture. Check the university library website for instructions on the use of its systems and pick
up the guide maps and instruction brochures when you are on campus.
Keep scanned copies of this information filed on your computer for easy
reference.

Research Strategy

Once you are familiar with the cataloguing systems and databases, continually map out and refine your **research strategy** so that you always
have an up-to-date plan of how you will solve problems and achieve your
research goals through efficient and effective use of your time and resources. Every good research strategy involves an organized, coherent,
and coordinated series of tactical moves designed to ensure that you find
and are able to access the materials that will allow you to gain a thorough
understanding of the state of knowledge in a specific area.

A research strategy involves multiple tactics for information-seeking and for developing critical skills. Information-seeking entails understanding what information you need, where to look for it, and how to use it effectively to solve problems. Critical thinking is involved as you continually assess the quality and usability of the materials you uncover. The ability to identify and evaluate sources is the most valuable skill a new researcher can develop.

Call Numbers and Browsing the Stacks

As you begin to identify promising subject areas and sources, you will likely notice that several books have similar **call numbers**. A good early step is to visit the university library and wander through the stacks. Browse the books on the shelf as you might look at related volumes in a bookstore. Look not only for the specific works you identified through the online system but also for related texts on the same subjects that are catalogued under similar call numbers.

The Library of Congress Classification is a system used in most North American libraries to organize books into different subject domains. After a letter, each book is given a number.

Subject Area Specialist Librarians

TABLE 1.1   THE LIBRARY OF CONGRESS CLASSIFICATION SYSTEM

A	General Works	L	Education
B	Philosophy, Psychology, Religion	M	Music and Books on Music
C	Auxiliary Sciences of History	N	Fine Arts
D	World History and History of Europe, Asia, Africa, Australia, New Zealand, etc.	P	Language and Literature
		Q	Science
E	History of the Americas	R	Medicine
F	History of the Americas	S	Agriculture
G	Geography, Anthropology, Recreation	T	Technology
H	Social Sciences	U	Military Science
J	Political Science	V	Naval Science
K	Law	Z	Bibliography, Library Science, Information Resources (General)

Many universities have subject area specialist librarians. You should be able to find a list of librarians with expertise in particular scholarly areas who can help you find documents that would be difficult to identify on your own. Asking for help from the specialist librarian is an important tactic for identifying a comprehensive batch of materials for your project.

Ranking Sources Based on Reliability and Trustworthiness

All sources are not equally valuable. There are three different levels and kinds of sources used in research: primary, secondary, and tertiary. Each kind has a place in your research strategy based on the reliability and trustworthiness of the information.

Primary Sources

Primary source material is typically raw data. For example, if you are concentrating on ethnographic studies, the statements and behaviours of the people at the centre of your research provide the raw material. If you are doing historical studies, raw data includes diaries of historical figures and documents from the time period. For philosophical studies, primary sources include the writings of a particular philosopher, often in the form of original manuscripts. The primary source data is typically more reliable and trustworthy than secondary or tertiary materials.

Still, following an initial reading of primary source material, you may find it helpful to look through secondary and tertiary sources in order to hone your ideas. Once you have a solid grasp of the subject area, return again to the primary source material and begin to look for evidence and ideas that support the argument and interpretation you are developing.

Secondary Sources

Secondary source materials discuss or interpret primary source material, that is, original information presented somewhere else. Secondary sources use raw data to solve research questions and provide commentary. They generalize, analyze, synthesize, interpret, or evaluate the original information. Peer-reviewed journal articles or chapters in edited collections, for example, often rely on secondary sources. In fact, you may well spend the bulk of your research time finding, reading, and assessing secondary sources for your research.

Tertiary Sources

Tertiary sources are books, articles, magazines, and other popular forms of information that synthesize the other two kinds of sources for general readers. Textbooks, encyclopedia articles, the top ten links from a Google search—these are all examples of tertiary materials. You can use these third-level sources to get a sense of your interests, to find a way into your topic, or to help you decide exactly what you want to do. Just be aware that tertiary sources are not the best way to support a scholarly argument because the information is typically general and sometimes oversimplified.

Finding the Research Strategy that Works for You

Some students find it helpful to begin with a Google search or a magazine article and then move on to Google Scholar and other peer-reviewed articles. Other students will begin with online databases or by talking to people. When you design your research strategy, just be sure to plan to focus the bulk of your attention on primary and secondary sources.

Learning to Search Online Databases

There are many tactics and techniques for identifying journals, eJournals, database lists, and other electronic resources available through your library. A general search will give you a sense of the material that is available. Are you finding thousands of entries? Try again using more specific search terms. Cannot find enough information? Use broader, more general terms.

Common Search Terms and Techniques

A number of terms and techniques can be used to make your search more effective. Not all university libraries make use of every technique, but using some of the most common ones will improve your ability to uncover a comprehensive search.

Synonyms
Use synonyms. The terms *chicken* and *poultry* will reveal very different kinds of research.

Different Spellings
Try multiple spellings. The terms *color* or *colour* may produce similar academic research, some produced in the United States and some in Canada or Britain. Pay attention to spelling errors. One ty#po can ruin a search.

Quotation Marks and Parentheses

Use quotation marks or parentheses to define phrases. For example, putting quotation marks around the phrase "a stitch in time saves nine" will limit your search to information with exactly this language. Use parentheses to group terms as you would in mathematical formulas—for example, *Prime Minister (Harper OR Trudeau)* or *communication technology (telephone AND telegraph)*.

Wildcards and Truncations

Certain punctuation marks or special symbols have particular meanings in different systems and function as wildcards or truncations.

Librarians use wildcard symbols such as the question mark (?) and the asterisk (*) when retrieving words that can be spelled in multiple ways. Wildcards allow you to substitute symbols for one or more letters. Wildcards are handy when you are uncertain of spelling, when there are alternate spellings, or when you only know part of a term. Different search engines employ various symbols, so you will need to check for exact instructions. For example, when carrying out a search on JSTOR, a widely used scholarly database, use a question mark (?) as a substitute for a missing character in a search term, when you are not certain of a spelling, or when you want to find two forms of one word. For example, *ne?t* will find *neat, nest,* and *next*.

Truncation allows you to search for a term and its variations. It involves adding a symbol at the end of a root word to retrieve all the variations of that word. In many North American databases, an asterisk (*) is the standard truncation symbol. For example, *Canad** will retrieve records containing *Canada, Canadians, Canada's,* and any other words that begin with those letters. However, on JSTOR, use the plus symbol (+) to truncate search terms and represent a single character, several characters, or no characters. For example, entering *pigment+* will find *pigment, pigments, pigmented, pigmentation,* and any other words beginning with *pigment*.

For plurals on JSTOR, use the ampersand (&). For example, *effect&* will find *effect* and *effects*.

Boolean Search Terms

Boolean searches are popular in all libraries and databases. The Boolean terms *AND, OR,* and *NOT* are capitalized. A Boolean search using the words *rocket* and *science,* for example, could be *rocket AND science* (which will include all items with *rocket* and *science*); *rocket OR science* (which will broaden the search to all items with either *rocket* or *science*); or *rocket NOT science* (which will narrow the search to sources that contain *rocket* but not *science*). All online search engines and databases currently use Boolean searches. In fact, Boolean logic is the simplest way to broaden or narrow your search.

Complex Search Strings

The most sophisticated search tactic is to construct complex strings that will zero in on information needed to answer your research question in the most direct way possible such as *microfinance AND Nepal NOT India AND farmers*. The more specific your search terms, the better the results.

Narrowing the Field

Make use of fields. All databases have fields such as date or publication type that help you limit your search.

Effectively using databases requires knowledge of the various search tactics as well as practice to see which particular techniques work best for your research area. When you learn to combine the techniques, you will have no problem uncovering the latest research.

Database Aggregators

Database aggregators gather together (i.e., aggregate) research articles from many different sources and journals. You can search multiple databases at the same time or work with a single database depending on your discipline or your area of inquiry. For example, the Arts and Humanities Citation Index aggregates more than 1,600 journals. EconLit—the American Economic Association database—aggregates more than 600 peer-reviewed and fully indexed journals on topics such as economic development, history, and macro- and microeconomics.

Subject Area or Discipline-Specific Databases

Universities typically organize their databases by subject or by discipline. Selecting by subject limits the number of databases for your keyword search. ProQuest and AMICUS are two of these databases.

ProQuest

ProQuest is one of the major database archives for newspapers, articles, and dissertations. Billions of pages of content are aggregated in its digital archive. ProQuest is also the official archive for dissertations and theses for the Library of Congress and the main database for graduate research around the world from 1861 to the present. By going through your university library database, you will have access to more than 1.2 million titles that are available for downloading. An additional 2 million copies are available for purchase if a thesis cannot be accessed over the Web.

AMICUS

Automated Management Information Civil Users System or AMICUS is another important database for Canadian students. AMICUS provides a free national catalogue that lists and offers access to all the holdings found in more than 1,300 Canadian libraries and at Library and Archives Canada.

Keywords

A crucial aspect of your research strategy involves identifying the most appropriate keywords. Certain words in our language open doorways to information. Keywords are important because they are used to index information in the catalogue or database search engine. The keywords you use will have a major impact on the number of relevant records you will find.

Basic Keyword Searches

Basic keyword searches are useful when you do not know the complete titles or names of authors. A basic keyword search allows you to combine two or more concepts, which will help you find more specific subject headings. In computer searches, success in identifying appropriate material depends on the quality, precision, and accuracy of keywords. Keywords evolve as you dig deeper into the material; expect to amend them throughout the research process.

Database Search Tactics

You can improve your search results by using the following strategies:

- choose the keywords you plan to use;
- brainstorm synonyms;
- identify terms most specific to the concepts;
- when you find relevant articles, examine them for potential new keywords;
- track what worked and what did not work so you do not repeat fruitless searches;
- use Boolean search terms: *AND, OR,* and *NOT*; and
- construct complex search strings using Boolean terms.

Searching the Internet

An Internet search is more general than research at your university library. Here again, all sources are not equal. Based on reliability and scholarly value, there are three broad categories of information found via Internet searches. These can be listed in descending order of reliability.

Peer-Reviewed Articles
The first and highest level of reliability belongs to open-source, peer-reviewed publications such as journal articles that are also available through your library website.

Results of a Standard Web Search
The second most reliable category is material gleaned from standard web searches, including information found through your search engine. When an article includes references to primary, secondary, or even tertiary sources, this information is more reliable than material that has not been edited, fact-checked, or peer-reviewed.

Marketing, Promotional, and Personal Sites
The third category involves less reliable information. This category of material concerns the content that individuals, corporations, businesses, and other groups have posted online in the form of blogs, articles, websites, and other digital forms. Typically, information generated from this general kind of web search has not undergone peer review. Nor have these sorts of online articles been subjected to systematic fact-checking. Without citations, referencing, and fact-checking, the information must be considered **hearsay**—the most dangerous source of information for any researcher.

Academic Integrity

Scholars have an obligation to act ethically in conducting research. What is at stake is academic integrity—the honesty, truthfulness, accuracy, and ethical standards you observe when pursuing your research. You must take responsibility for conducting your research in accordance with the highest ethical standards. If you cheat, the penalties are severe.

The most effective way to avoid cheating is to give yourself enough time to acquire skills, study, write, and do the work. Build this time into your schedule by creating a timeline as part of your research strategy. Cheating often occurs when students do not have enough time to complete an assignment by the deadline and they are so desperate to avoid failing that they are willing to risk losing everything. This is why it is important for you to set realistic, achievable goals and to schedule your time wisely. If you are not clear about what actions are considered cheating, participate in the instructional sessions offered by your library and take this information to heart.

Timelines

To create a timeline, download a good calendar. Keep in mind all of the projects and activities in your life that will demand your attention while you conduct your research. Block out in advance the time you will need to do the work. Schedule a few hours for your research on as many days as you think it will take for you to master the material and complete the best work of which you are capable.

Time management experts point out that being effective is not so much about making time in your schedule for your research as it is prioritizing the research in your schedule. Think about giving yourself a set amount of time to do the initial research within the overall timeframe you have to complete the assignment. You can get tripped up and spend a disproportionate amount of your energy working on the initial phase rather than putting the emphasis on the later developments of the research. Building a timeline is a key element in circumventing procrastination, creating strong study habits, and avoiding copying and cheating as last-ditch efforts to keep yourself from failing.

FINAL CHECKLIST

- ○ Perform a preliminary Internet search to uncover parameters and significant sources of information.
- ○ Go to the university library website and search the online catalogue.
- ○ Select a few keywords to help focus your general search.
- ○ Learn how to use online journal databases to identify major journals, associations, and other resources.
- ○ Make an appointment with your subject area specialist librarian.
- ○ Browse the stacks.
- ○ Look for influential authors that others cite.

○ Apply keyword, author, and title searches to these selected resources.

○ Begin creating a bibliography to keep track of the resources you discover.

○ Evaluate material based on its reliability, trustworthiness, and intellectual value.

○ Try writing in complete sentences as you generate ideas.

○ Explore digital tools and how they might connect to your keywords.

○ Make a realistic timeline.

Chapter Summary

This chapter explained some of the differences between producing a print document and researching and creating a project that integrates scholarship and new media. We also pointed to ways that digital technologies are challenging long-standing patterns of scholarly production. We presented guidelines for using library and Internet resources and suggested how you might identify preliminary search terms. We also asked you to make your research a priority by creating a timeline, and we underscored the importance of ethical conduct in research.

2

Finding and Narrowing
a Topic

Chapter Outline

Chapter Two helps you find and narrow a topic and begin thinking about
your digital project. To aid with the process of generating ideas and
structuring your topic and project, we offer advice on techniques such as free
association, brainstorming, and cognitive mapping. We also help you begin
thinking about your digital media project and the elements necessary for its
design. Our checklist helps you choose and delineate a topic.

Getting Started

Where to begin? One of the most difficult aspects of researching, writing, and creating a project is identifying a subject that both ignites your passion and meets your instructor's criteria for the essay, thesis, or capstone project.

Did you particularly enjoy researching a subject in the past? Were you intrigued by a topic from a previous course? Have you read a book, chapter, or journal article that excited you? Is there a documentary film or television show that has captured your interest? Did a recent newspaper or magazine article describe an event, action, or discovery that you would like to explore in more detail?

Talk to your instructors, fellow students, family, and friends about your ideas. Record your thoughts in a notebook or journal. Talking and writing about your ideas will help you to zero in on interests that you would like to research.

Selecting a Research Topic

The term *topic* comes from the Greek word *topos*, meaning place or location. Finding a topic at this preliminary stage in your research involves locating your subject within a discipline or at the intersection of two or more disciplines, narrowing it further by placing it within a subdiscipline or specialization, and then subdividing the topic further still into its component ideas, evidence, and arguments.

Finding a Topic Quickly

The earlier you are able to identify a focused topic, the more time you will have to work on your project. Students often have difficulty identifying a research area that meshes their particular interests with established bodies of academic research, and so they spend valuable time weighing various options for topics—time that would have been better spent on other aspects of their study.

Your goal is to find an interesting and challenging research area in a reasonably short time period. The sooner you identify a topic, the sooner you can commence the research. Once you focus on a specific area, you can continue to narrow the topic as you begin your research.

Finding a Scholarly Niche

Your level of interest in the subject area will determine the amount of effort and enthusiasm you put into your research. Working on a topic that arouses your curiosity and sense of wonder is the first step in identifying an area of research that will keep you going even during times of frustration or slow progress.

Finding a Compelling and Manageable Topic

You need to select a topic that is manageable yet provides many different avenues for exploration. These are related goals. If topics are very new, specialized, or technical, there may be a limited range of source materials for your research. Make sure your topic has a strong literature base in peer-reviewed academic books and articles so you have a wide variety of materials to fuel your study. If you find few materials that resemble your proposed idea, then maybe it is not the best topic for your project.

Narrowing the Topic

Many students have the opposite problem—the number of books and articles available in a subject area overwhelms them. You may be able to identify a general direction but have more difficulty narrowing your lens of inquiry onto a particular topic that is achievable.

There are a number of ways you might go about narrowing your topic. What follows are some suggestions for how you might delimit your study.

Subdisciplines within a Discipline

Find out how professionals divide a discipline into subdisciplines. Manageable topics typically fall into a small section of a subdiscipline of a larger category of research.

Programs and Handbooks Offered by Disciplinary Departments

Examine a number of university department websites and handbooks. Look at the programs they list. The division into university departments often mirrors established disciplinary boundaries; the list of programs reflects the subdisciplines in a field. Search the programs and specializations at several institutions to get a good grasp of the divisions, subdivisions, and specializations in a discipline.

Education, for example, is typically organized into ten to fifteen sub-disciplines, including (1) arts in education; (2) education, policy, and management; (3) higher education; (4) human development and psychology; (5) international education policy; (6) language and literacy; (7) learning and teaching; (8) mind, brain, and education; (9) school leadership; (10) special studies; (11) teacher education; and (12) technology, innovation, and education.

Are you interested in an interdisciplinary topic that combines two or more established disciplines? Examine the collaborative programs offered by a department. Collaborative programs can serve as a guide to interdisciplinary areas that are moving into the mainstream in the academy.

Biographies and Research Interests of Professors in a Department

When you have a sense of the divisions and specializations in your general subject area, look at how professors in a department describe their research areas and interests on the university website.

The specializations of the professors in smaller departments generally indicate the areas of research that are regarded as core to a discipline; small departments cannot afford to have a professor for every subdivision in a discipline, so they must focus on the basics. Larger departments can afford to have professors for more of the subject areas that make up a discipline, and therefore the interests and research of these professors provide a better sense of the full range of specializations.

Textbooks as a Guide to Disciplinary Subdivisions

Go to the university bookstore and look at the textbooks in your discipline. The divisions into chapters of first-year undergraduate textbooks are organized into the various branches of a discipline. In contrast to textbooks for introductory courses, which provide an overview of the entire discipline, the chapter divisions in textbooks for upper-level undergraduate and master's level courses set forth the divisions of the subdisciplines or specializations within the discipline.

Turn to the list of references provided by these textbooks. Textbooks most often reference key studies that have shaped the discipline and its specializations as well as the recent essays and books of the most prominent and influential thinkers. The titles of publications in each area can serve as guides and models for narrowing your own research.

Associations, Conference Abstracts, and Proceedings

Consult the websites of the various scholarly associations in your field. Associations hold annual conferences and post calls for papers. These calls provide insight into the topics at the forefront of new research in a discipline. Since disciplinary associations hope to attract broad participation and attendance at meetings, the themes and panels listed in the calls typically hold interest for many members.

Associations also make available lists of abstracts from conferences and often publish proceedings (the papers that were presented at various panels at a meeting). These documents will give you a good sense of the topics and themes on the leading edge of a discipline, and so one of these subjects would be an excellent choice for your research project.

Identify a Topic by Finding a Problem or Asking a Question

Another approach to finding a topic is to think of your project as responding to a problem or question rather than researching a field. What bodies of research will you need to investigate and integrate in order to respond appropriately to your problem or question? Read widely in these bodies of research and begin writing an initial plan. Then do more reading, flesh out your plan, revise it, and then do more reading still. Your plan only needs to be provisional at this stage—you continue to revise it as you make progress through your project.

Vision and Revision

Again, research is not a linear process. An essay project involves envisioning a finished product and then shifting back and forth in your mind's eye between the work you have accomplished and what needs to be done in order to realize your vision. This process is continuous throughout the project.

Every time your reading and research reveals something new, you examine the ideas you wrote previously and set about revising your study. With every revision, you bring more clarity and precision to your writing so that your document—paper or electronic—gradually moves in the direction of your vision for the final piece.

In fact, many scholars are convinced that narrowing a topic involves continuous reading, writing, and thinking. Do enough research to become familiar with your subject areas, and then start laying down tracks in a first draft. When you begin writing, set yourself a target, say 500 to 1,000 words per day. Even if this initial material has to be extensively revised, you will make progress. There is also a psychological advantage to working with a first draft—you will no longer be staring at a blank page. It is easier to edit and improve a draft than it is to formulate sentences and paragraphs from scratch.

What Is the Rationale or Purpose for Your Research?

As you begin writing, keep your rationale in mind at all times. Why are you bothering with this research, and why should readers make an effort to look at it? Why is your study important? What is at issue? What will happen if nothing is done? What is at stake in this research?

Your rationale should guide the framing of your question, establish a context for the project, clarify the relationship between your topic and previous research, and justify your selection of evidence and the methods you will use to carry out your analysis, including your digital design.

The relationship between past work in a discipline or subdiscipline and your topic is important to your rationale. Having a clear purpose will also help to focus and direct your reading and research.

Brainstorming: Four Strategies for Identifying a Topic

Brainstorming is an informal approach to the task and challenge of finding a topic. The objective is to try to generate thoughts, ideas, questions, and reflections that may appear at first to be incongruous, incoherent, or unrelated. The aim is to spark your imagination and get you thinking outside of the box. Be open to anything that comes to mind and jot down your thoughts. Do not be critical of your ideas. Negative judgments inhibit the process. At the end of the brainstorming process, apply analysis, judgment, and critical thinking to your ideas, identify the best ones, and then formulate your next steps.

Here are four strategies for brainstorming that can help get you started. These do not follow in sequence, and you may try only one technique or all of them. The point is to stimulate your thinking beyond your first thoughts in order to help you get to the crux of where your interests actually lie.

Technique One: Bibliographic Methods

Identify three to five related subject areas, disciplines, subdisciplines, or fields that seem aligned with your interests. Begin to find source materials and look them over to locate the best peer-reviewed research.

Then start developing the bibliography with style guide in hand. If you create your list of works cited manually, it is more efficient to check the style guide for the correct format as you input each entry, rather than waiting to format all entries just before you submit your project. Even if your bibliography has been created automatically with a citation program such as RefWorks, you will need to double-check the format of every entry. Citation software creates many glitches and inconsistencies that will need to be corrected by hand.

Write out the names of the sources you have identified, looking for linkages, overlaps, and keywords. Ascertain whether or not certain bodies of research will be sufficient or even adequate as starting points for your reading. As your bibliography begins to take shape, you will find that the collection of works you have developed starts to tell a story. This story can be fleshed out more fully as you proceed with the writing.

Technique Two: Finding Problems and Asking Questions

What do you want to know? You can start with a random question and then examine your reasons for seeking answers to the question. For example, you can ask, "What can be done to reduce poverty in this country?" You could do considerable research and develop a "doable" project on addressing poverty.

But chances are, the first question that comes to your mind will not encapsulate what you really want to know. Nor will it be the exact problem you want to spend the next few months investigating.

Try making a long list of problems or questions. Look for connections among them in order to winnow out the important ideas from material that is tangential or extraneous. Circle the three to five problems or questions that best reflect your intellectual interests and then concentrate on revising and refining them so they more fully reflect the project you would like to investigate.

Technique Three: Dialogue

Have a dialogue with yourself about the project and write down this self-conversation. The Greek philosopher Plato instructs that "thinking is the dialogue the mind carries out with itself in silence."

Be of two minds. One mind is critical; it breaks problems into parts and analyzes them. The other is creative; it seeks wholeness and unity. The critical mindset concentrates on analysis: What confuses you? What needs changing? Where are the injustices in a system? What is not working? What are the problems? What are the hidden assumptions? Where are the gaps in our understanding? The creative mindset focuses on synthesis: Where do I see connections? What are the issues about which everyone agrees? What makes sense to me? If I boil down all these arguments, what do they all seem to be saying? This internal dialoguing exercise applies a process of metacognition to the challenge of finding and narrowing your topic.

Metacognition is the term for higher order thinking. It is "thinking about thinking." Writing out your self-dialogue will give you a record of this process. Train yourself to critically examine your thoughts as you experience them. Gaining control over your thoughts or cognitions is key to learning. By writing out your self-dialogue, you will have a written record of how you have been "thinking about your thinking."

RESEARCH IN ACTION · Hanna's story

Hanna knew she was interested in *Second Life*—the 3D virtual world that people play online. She was not sure how to turn this interest into a research idea. She began by looking at research databases and discovered studies in computer science, communication studies, psychology, and sociology that dealt with virtual worlds. Her investigation confirmed that there were enough studies on these topics to keep her from struggling due to a lack of research.

Hanna then made a list of all the things she wanted to know about *Second Life*. She tried various techniques of free association, brainstorming, and internal dialoguing about all of her possible interests. Through this process, she discovered that she was most interested in the choices people make when creating a unique avatar and how these choices affected the interactions with other avatars in the virtual world. She recalled her interest in health care and began to focus her research questions about how *Second Life* might function as an adaptive resource for people with physical disabilities.

At this point, Hanna realized that she had narrowed her topic sufficiently to begin her research in earnest. Having identified a solid topic, she knew she could continue to refine it as her research progressed.

Technique Four: Free Association

Making no attempts to concentrate, report your thoughts without editing them. This technique is based upon two assumptions. The first assumption is that all lines of thought have the potential to lead to something significant. The second assumption is that the relaxation that comes from free association maximizes your ability to concentrate.

Set yourself a goal of writing one hundred possible ideas. Jot down your first thoughts and then follow your chain of associations and see where they lead you. Print this list and begin a process of analysis by circling or drawing arrows to related ideas.

Look for overlaps and identify repetitions. From your list of a hundred ideas, identify the most promising ones and see if you can reduce them to about ten likely topics that can serve as possible starting points.

Moving from Your Interests to a Topic

As you zero in on the topics that might serve as the focus of your investigation, the next step is to begin to organize and structure your thoughts. Cognitive mapping and the inverted pyramid will help you with this stage.

Cognitive Mapping

Cognitive mapping is a writing exercise that helps you organize, categorize, and find themes among your various ideas. This process allows you to visualize a vast collection of ideas and will help you to lay out a larger plan. It also helps you to identify subcategories and relationships among themes, to structure messy and complex data for problem solving, and to manage a large number of ideas. The point of cognitive mapping is that it helps you to apply structure to a number of randomly arranged ideas.

Cognitive mapping exercises can also indicate where the core issues lie. Dilemmas, feedback loops, and conflicts can be identified, explored, and investigated. The exercises can also be adapted and applied to help you isolate chunks of ideas and work out a chain of arguments. As well, the exercises help simplify the complexity of your thinking and provide keywords for future literature searches.

Creating a cognitive map involves four main steps:

1. Write your main idea in the centre of a sheet of paper and draw a shape around it such as a circle, square, or triangle. Then draw lines radiating outwards to sub-ideas. There is no wrong way to

develop a cognitive map. Some resemble webs, while others look like mazes, family trees, labyrinths, or surveyor maps.

2. When you have indicated a number of sub-ideas, draw arrows that connect one idea to another. Try to consider how some ideas are more abstract while others are more concrete. Examine the relationships among your ideas and sub-ideas and then redraw your chart, refining these relationships. For clarity, you might try keeping the most abstract ideas in the centre of your page with the arrows moving outwards to more concrete or solid notions.

3. Think about how some of the circled ideas might be related, and draw ladders or feedback loops to signify relationships among your various topics, ideas, and concepts.

4. Write out short notes that explain some of the arrows. Use these notes to identify three or more major categories that help you frame your research ideas.

The point of the cognitive mapping exercise is to identify major themes and sub-themes, that is, the categories for further analysis. You will also be able to separate out ideas that you really like but that you need to exclude so as to make your research more coherent or doable. This exercise should help you structure your ideas and should provide you with the key

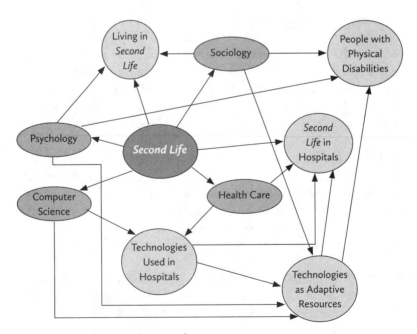

Sample cognitive map, based on Hanna's story.

elements and words so that you are ready to write a general plan for your next step of the research.

Inverted Pyramid

The inverted pyramid is a technique for organizing and prioritizing information. It is commonly used by journalists to formulate news stories. The technique can also be used to focus your scholarly inquiry in ways that begin with general areas of interest and move gradually to more specific topics.

The inverted pyramid can be envisioned as a triangle or an arrowhead pointing downwards on a page. In other words, the triangle is positioned on the page so that the wide part forms a horizontal line at the top and the shape tapers downwards to the point at the bottom. In the journalistic model, the most important, salient, or interesting aspects of the information are allocated to the widest part of the triangle, indicating that this material should head the article. As the triangle gradually narrows to a point, the information and details follow in order of decreasing importance.

To start your inverted pyramid, think of something general about your subject matter. For example, you may be aware that in the field of political science, scholars have long been asking questions about the nature and

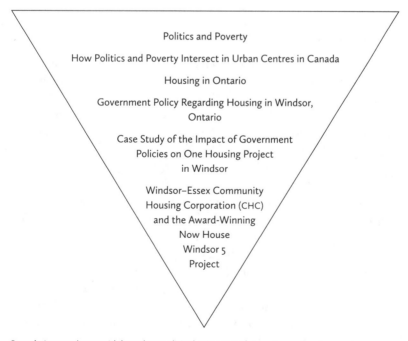

Politics and Poverty

How Politics and Poverty Intersect in Urban Centres in Canada

Housing in Ontario

Government Policy Regarding Housing in Windsor, Ontario

Case Study of the Impact of Government Policies on One Housing Project in Windsor

Windsor–Essex Community Housing Corporation (CHC) and the Award-Winning Now House Windsor 5 Project

Sample inverted pyramid, based on political science and poverty.

ramifications of poverty, so you might focus on finding material in political science related to poverty. Then you narrow the lens further so that the second part of the pyramid focuses on specifics such as the politics of poverty in Canadian urban settings. Delimit further, for example, to liberal politics, urban poverty, and community-supported housing in Ontario.

Such processes of organizing your thoughts can lead to a very specific project—in this case to a study of one particular community housing project, the award-winning Now House Windsor 5 project in Windsor, Ontario, and its adoption of government policies concerning social support.

A Refined Topic and Its Components

Once you have completed these brainstorming and mapping exercises, it is time to begin to put together a clear and coherent outline for what will become your Introduction and Review of Literature.

The components of any topic must be organized in order and be in the right proportions for the length of your study. The organization and the size of the different parts of your study will begin to emerge as you continue with your literature searches and get more fully into the writing.

Recipe or Formula for Your Topic

Think of this outlining process as an activity similar to conducting a science experiment or cooking a simple recipe, which involves organizing your ingredients, measuring them accurately and in the right proportions, and combining them in a certain order or by way of a particular procedure. The proportions and the method for combining them determine the final product.

The Topic Outline

The outline of your topic and project must include the components and the methods you will use to ensure that your final product comes together and stands up against other research in your field.

Spend time reviewing your outline and thinking about how the various elements relate to other elements as a cohesive whole. Consider how your component parts might function as headings, subheadings, or points for your later writing. These will evolve as you continue researching and writing, but putting the components and approach into words will help you make rapid progress in structuring your thinking.

Creating a Structure

To build an ordered structure, keep your outline moving from general topics to more specific details—or reverse that process and move from the specific instance to the more general. Avoid jumping from one abstract idea to a tangential thought. Ideas should be connected through smooth transitions and carefully constructed logic.

A well-organized outline helps you see the arguments that are beginning to take shape from your research. The logic behind the organization of your components eventually forms the logic of your argument.

Topic to Problem

As you narrow the general topic to a specific research topic, begin to identify problems that occur at the intersection of the various bodies of knowledge. As you continue to read, note the issues about which there is widespread agreement. What are the puzzles that scholars identify? What do a number of the researchers find perplexing? What are the opposing views? Why do different scholars hold such differing perspectives? What is at issue? Is it simply a different reading of the same evidence? If so, is the evidence assigned different weights by the various scholars? Or do different researchers cite different evidence altogether to support their position?

Problem statements often provide a synopsis of the topic as a whole. From a technical point of view, this involves **empirical investigation**— that is, data collection and analysis. The quality of your answers to your problem will help determine the precise type of research question and creative project that you will create.

Problem to Question

The next step involves refining your topic further to frame a research question. Rely on the problem and the draft questions you developed earlier, and begin focusing and framing one excellent query sentence. Consider the two or three bodies of research you are bringing together in the literature review.

One technique that works in many cases is to restate your general inquiry in a form that reads "What is the relationship between x and y?" Relationship questions help you find the areas of overlap between different bodies of knowledge.

Key Terms

The key terms you use in your question become focal terms in your study; you will probably want to define them and use them to carry out further library searches. The key terms need to be divided into more detailed ideas, which will then form some of the subheadings for your outline.

Assumptions Encapsulated in the Problem Statement and Research Question

The chief point in finding a problem or asking a question is to see what kinds of information you will have to identify in order to develop an adequate response. Carefully examine the way you formulate the problem or phrase the question—the problem and question encapsulate a number of hidden assumptions that you will need to make explicit.

Assumptions function as hidden frameworks that shape our basic ideas and understanding of the state of affairs. These assumptions may not be accurate. The point of exposing your own hidden assumptions is to bring your critical thinking to the foreground so that you are able to see the prejudices and biases that may lead you astray in your investigation.

Question to Hypothesis

Your problem and question help shape your hypothesis. The hypothesis is the first stage in developing a thesis statement. In the early stages of the research, it is not possible to create a firm thesis statement. The thesis emerges from the research, and since you have not yet carried out your research of the literature, gathered and analyzed your data, or determined the findings or results of your investigation, you must hold off on the thesis statement until a later stage in the research.

The hypothesis will stand in for the thesis at this early stage. Depending on your topic, it may remain as a key part of your Introduction in the final study.

In one or two sentences, the hypothesis statement offers a guess at what you think your research will show. Hypotheses also indicate the ways you might go about testing the thesis.

Hypothesis to Position

As you limit the research to a particular problem, question, and tentative hypothesis, keep in mind that your goal is to persuade your reader—using an argument supported by evidence and logical reasoning—to accept the position you have taken.

In the context of the digital essay, the term *argument* has two meanings. The first is when you take a side in a debate. For example, you might argue for or against controversial issues such as censorship, abortion, or the death penalty. The second meaning of argument—rather simply—is to make a case. When you take a position on an issue, you need to defend it using persuasive evidence. In taking a stand in support of one position over other possible views, your essay will make a claim. You present the arguments and evidence that will convince your reader that your claims are warranted so that they come around to your view. This claim is supported by evidence that you have discovered through your research process.

As you progress with the research, continually ask yourself "What is my own point of view on the problem and debates? What do I think? What is my research suggesting? Based on the research, which side of the discussion do I support? What will I argue? How will I weigh and use the evidence I am finding to support my position?"

Problem, Argument, Counterargument, and Evidence

Evidence substantiates, verifies, confirms, and lends credence to the position you take with respect to the problem. Sound arguments rely on evidence to convince a reader that there is merit to your argument and substance to your claims.

As you think about taking a side, try to anticipate counterarguments and opposing views that might be offered in support of an alternative position. What evidence can you offer that rebuts these alternative views? Avoiding counterarguments and counterclaims is a logical fallacy and a sure way to raise doubts in your reader's mind about your position. Readers are persuaded to adopt your position when you offer good reasons for doing so. You should acknowledge the arguments and evidence that go against the position you are taking and provide reasons why they are not accurate or should not be given priority. Your reasoning should be backed up by evidence that is intelligently interpreted and deployed. In anticipating arguments from the other side of the issue, your aim is to show how the weight of evidence supports your side.

Creative Project Design

To further conceptualize your topic, you need to consider the overall design of your creative project as well. Think about whether you might want to make a podcast, video, or website as you move through these stages of finding and developing a topic. There are many media examples that are available for collection. Begin to gather, store, and organize these materials. One media text might work as a starting place, but as you engage in research and develop a more refined topic, you will want to review additional media.

Some kinds of arguments lend themselves to particular forms of media. For example, the techniques of documentary film are often linked to ethnographic research and interviewing strategies, and web design effectively communicates different levels and kinds of information through images, texts, and sounds. You are only limited by your imagination.

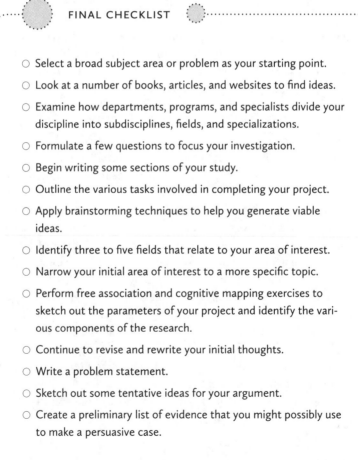

FINAL CHECKLIST

- ○ Select a broad subject area or problem as your starting point.
- ○ Look at a number of books, articles, and websites to find ideas.
- ○ Examine how departments, programs, and specialists divide your discipline into subdisciplines, fields, and specializations.
- ○ Formulate a few questions to focus your investigation.
- ○ Begin writing some sections of your study.
- ○ Outline the various tasks involved in completing your project.
- ○ Apply brainstorming techniques to help you generate viable ideas.
- ○ Identify three to five fields that relate to your area of interest.
- ○ Narrow your initial area of interest to a more specific topic.
- ○ Perform free association and cognitive mapping exercises to sketch out the parameters of your project and identify the various components of the research.
- ○ Continue to revise and rewrite your initial thoughts.
- ○ Write a problem statement.
- ○ Sketch out some tentative ideas for your argument.
- ○ Create a preliminary list of evidence that you might possibly use to make a persuasive case.

○ Make a list of possible counterarguments to the position you are taking so you can anticipate objections and mount evidence that shows your view to be more accurate.

○ Imagine how you might connect these initial ideas to a potential digital project.

Chapter Summary

This chapter explained how to find a topic and then break it down into its various components. We suggested ways to narrow your investigation so that you find a focused topic for research. Free association, brainstorming, and cognitive mapping exercises helped you to generate and organize your topic and project. You also started visualizing your digital media project and the elements necessary for its design. The next three chapters will help you identify the digital tools and techniques that you will use for your research and digital essay.

3

An Ecology of Digital Tools and Tactics

Chapter Outline

As you continue with the research and begin to narrow a topic, you should also be exploring the possibilities of digital design. The next three chapters describe digital media tools that can be used to enhance your scholarship and to create your digital essay. In this chapter, we explain how using tools such as blogs, wikis, microblogs, and aggregators can become integral to your scholarly productivity. In Chapters Four and Five, we briefly describe some of the tools and techniques that are currently available, emphasizing that new platforms come online regularly and older ones fall out of use. At the end of these three chapters, you will have extended your digital vocabulary, developed media competency, and become familiar with the tools and techniques you might use. Then, in Chapter Six, we begin writing and creating the digital project.

Blogging

Weblogs or **blogs** are websites that are easy to create and update even if you possess minimal technological know-how. Blogs can take the form of online diaries, journalism articles (known as grassroots journalism), thematically focused commentaries on current events or particular topics, curriculum vitae or resumés summarizing expertise in a field and promoting an individual or group, or they can be used for external communication and outreach to a wider community by scholars, politicians, analysts, artists, or business people.

Some bloggers film themselves speaking directly to viewers, which they then post. This is known as a **vlog** (video blog).

The defining feature of blogs is that they include a time-stamped entry format and a reverse chronological order filing system, so the most recent posting appears first. In addition to text, blogs may feature audio, pictures, and video; they can also store other files for linking. Most blogs also have interactive features such as **blogrolls** (links to other blogs that the owner reads or follows), comments, or trackbacks, that make it possible to communicate with other blogs.

RSS Feeds

Blogs have **RSS feeds** that support tracking updates. RSS—an initialism standing for Really Simple Syndication or Rich Site Summary—is a system for publishing content that is changed or updated on a regular basis.

Metadata

Blog entries and online news reports have RSS feeds that include either full text or summaries of content, plus **metadata** (information about the data such as publishing dates, authorship, purpose, or location on a network). ◐

Web Syndication

RSS feeds allow those who want to publish their work frequently to distribute content from one site to many other sites automatically, a process known as **syndication**. Web syndication ensures that a notice about updated content is sent to subscribers so that they are aware of changes to their favourite sites. If you want to receive updates from a number of different sources, RSS channels notices from many blogs or websites into the inbox on your computer. We present a more detailed explanation of RSS feeds and syndication below.

Extensible Markup Language (XML)

Blogs also use a standardized Extensible Markup Language (XML) file format that defines the rules for encoding documents so they can be read by both people and computers. XML makes it possible for the information on the site to be published and viewed by many different programs. You do not need to know XML in order to create a blog because many blogging programs automatically use XML.

Why Are Blogs So Popular?

Though blogs have existed since the middle of the 1990s, their usage has increased exponentially in the last five years. The website Technorati estimates that one out of six people has a personal blog (Technorati 2011). There are good reasons for the popularity of blogs.

Ease of Publication

Publishing a blog is easy; there is no need to learn code, and in many cases no hosting setup is required. To update your blog, you just log in to the site from any Internet connection, type the content on a typical Internet form, and hit Enter.

Blogs Create Communities

Blogs are also a form of social software that tends to foster a sense of community among users. Many blogs allow comments on entries and create a virtual forum for interaction among readers and respondents. Blogs encourage discussion. A visitor to your blog might communicate with you and with others who read and post with regularity, creating a sense of belonging and a shared perspective.

Blogs Provide Links to Other Resources

The blog's content management system makes it possible to provide links to other web resources, including other blogs, via permalinks—that is, individual addresses. Pingback and trackback features (methods for web authors to be notified when someone links to one of their documents) allow one blogger to notify another blogger of changes, thereby facilitating inter-blog conversation.

The Blogosphere

The term *blogosphere* refers to this interlinking of blogs, bloggers, and readers posting comments. For example, politically savvy Internet users often rely on blogs before they consult any other news source. Convenience, community, and rapid information are all features that account for so many users of the blog format, and make blogs an excellent tool for communicating your scholarly interests with like-minded others. ◉

Blogs for Research

There is no question that blogs are a valuable tool for the dissemination of research. You can use a blog to generate commentary on your research, your discipline, or your university.

Blogs as a Discussion Forum or Laboratory

Commentaries on blog entries can serve as a discussion forum or as a sort of semi-public laboratory where scientific hypotheses are tested. Since blog entries always have a permanent link together with a record of the posting date, they also provide a record of the scientific process.

Public Blogs

Public blogs open new avenues to the ivory tower. When used as a tool for public outreach, blogs can inform the wider community about new findings. In this way, they can be used to foster better public understanding of scholarship.

Prepublication

Blogs also offer a form of prepublication. Have you discovered something new and want to test the water with others in your discipline before heading off to a conference? The commentary function provides you with an open peer-review procedure for quality control.

Data and Information Collection

Yet another use for your blog is as a tool for collecting information scattered across various web platforms. Within research groups, this collection could take the form of joint blogs, which provide another possible platform for collaboration.

Blogs as Research Journals

In addition, a blog can be a learning journal that accompanies you throughout the writing of your final project. It can serve as an informal way of publishing or discussing your preliminary findings, recording decisive moments in the development of your project, and documenting in diary form the progress of a term paper, thesis, or capstone project.

Raising Your Research Profile

Finally, as many avid bloggers can attest, posting regularly can help establish your research profile, get your work read, and ensure that other scholars see your research (Nentwich 2010). See the companion website for examples of useful blogs that communicate information. ◉

Wikis for Collaboration

A **wiki** is "a system that allows one or more people to build up a corpus of knowledge in a set of interlinked web pages, using a process of creating and editing pages" (Franklin and Van Harmelen 2007, 5). In other words, a wiki is a website that can be accessed and edited by a number of people, thus facilitating collaborative work.

Wikis have a variety of unique and powerful features for information-sharing and collaboration. Users can add content to particular texts, create hyperlinks to and from other web pages, or post comments and questions that in turn create new pages. Several authors can work jointly on texts on a user-friendly web platform, gradually improving and extending others' contributions. Wikis also function as sources of information and knowledge and as tools for collaborative authoring.

Advantages of Wikis

One of the great advantages of wikis is that they have no predefined structure or organizational format, making them effective for group projects that entail collaborative writing and especially for those that include other kinds of digital tools.

Wikis also provide a document tool that allows a community to record group knowledge on topics of shared interest. Another advantage is that wikis provide an economical way to communicate and collaborate. Since it is easy to work with wikis, there are few technological barriers to their use. They also provide a number of functions, making them superior to voice or e-mail for collaboration, constructive learning, and knowledge production.

In fact, wikis have attributes that scholars have identified as being fundamental to a successful community of practice, including the following:

- opportunities for a variety of types of interactions;
- easy participation;
- connections to broader subject fields;
- the creation of personal and community identity;

- democratic forms of involvement; and
- the ability to evolve over time (Schwartz et al. 2004).

Since wikis allow researchers to meet virtually when it is convenient and to work on projects together, a geographically dispersed team can keep in touch, receive updates, and share ideas as the project develops.

Studies have found that the way wikis consolidate comments and ideas on one web page provides a clearer picture of a team's direction than individual e-mail messages (Naish 2006). In other words, it is more efficient to post an update to a wiki than to e-mail files from one individual to each member of the group, and then attempt to synthesize the edits. See the companion website for a list of useful and popular wikis. ◉⟩

HyperText Markup Language (HTML)

Wikis have functions that allow contributors to add and edit content via any web browser without prior knowledge of HyperText Markup Language (HTML), the system that allows pages to be displayed in a web browser. HTML is used to tag text and images in angle brackets <html> so that a web browser can read the document and organize it into a web page. The HTML tags are invisible from the web page; the browser does not display them but rather uses HTML tags to interpret the content of the page.

The Wiki as a Learning Tool and Knowledge Base

Wikis are great tools for group authoring because they draw members of a project together and allow them to build and edit a document on a single, central wiki page. Once research is underway, the wiki becomes the prime learning tool and knowledge base for the project. You can use a wiki to map concepts, to brainstorm, to produce a linked network of resources, and for collaborative concept elaboration.

The Wiki as a Record of a Project's History

Since wikis record changes and keep extensive page histories, they facilitate and promote close reading, revision, and tracking of work on an ongoing basis (Lamb 2004). If crucial material is deleted by mistake, or if inaccurate or unsuitable material is posted, it is possible to view the edits and roll back the pages to retrieve a previous version of the document.

The Wiki as a Project Monitoring Tool

Since a wiki records work continually and serves as a document of previous decisions involving content or procedure, new members who join a team mid-project can catch up on the state of group knowledge by browsing the site. Wikis often provide tools that allow members of the user community to monitor the changing state of the wiki so that any issues that emerge can be discussed.

Wikis allow you to grasp the big picture and take action before problems become acute. Ever wonder what went wrong with a project? A wiki will allow members to go back and survey the overall arc and trajectory of the research to pinpoint areas that can be improved for the next major undertaking.

Using a wiki as a writing tool maximizes the advantages that can be gained from reflection, reviewing, publication, and the constant revision of written results (Fountain 2005). Team members can share thoughts on the research process itself. Or individuals can comment on journal articles, thereby contributing to the creation of a collaborative annotated bibliography. In the information age, if your project entails a group presentation or collaborative work, wikis are almost a necessity. Nearly everyone is familiar with Wikipedia.

Limitations of Wikis

Though anyone can read and edit a wiki, they do have some limitations. Most wikis require users to register and log in to read and edit documents, restricting access to members of a community. Some wikis are hosted on internal servers that are not accessible through the Internet. And not all wikis are free; some wiki hosting sites that cater to the business community demand a fee for usage.

Wikis also have fewer layout options in comparison with word processing software. In many cases, the document will have to be copied from the wiki to a word processing document for final polishing and formatting.

In addition, for students or team members working in different geographic locations seeking to jointly author or co-author a study, the wiki may prove slightly cumbersome. While each member can add content, it is not possible for people viewing the site from other locations to see what another person is writing as they are writing. The writer must hit Save and post the material to the Internet before others can read their edits. So while simultaneous writing would be ideal in some circumstances, members have to take turns writing and editing content.

Overall though, wikis are great tools for developing a project, creating a project plan collaboratively, and documenting everyone's contribution. You and your collaborators can rely on the wiki to track progress, generate reports, and record your work on assigned tasks.

Wikis versus Blogs

Wikis have frequently been compared to blogs because both are easy to create, maintain, and continually publish content. Indeed, they are both great tools for disseminating information as well as for getting feedback from the public. There are, however, noteworthy differences between blogs and wikis, chiefly in the way that they organize information, in the number of contributors they can support, and in what the contributors are able to achieve (Doyle 2006).

Collaboration versus Sole Authorship

Whereas wikis are designed for collaborative authoring by everyone, blogs are more personal and are generally written by a single author.

Organization by Topic or Reverse Chronology

Wikis organize information into topics. By contrast, blogs organize information in reverse chronological order. Topics in wikis are expected to evolve and often expand into something of a permanent knowledge base; the information in blogs is more of a historical record. Though wikis may not always display the order in which information was documented, it is very easy to browse and find related information. The reverse chronological order of blogs makes it more difficult to browse all postings on a particular topic.

Linked References versus New Posting

Likewise, the blog format is not as well suited as a wiki in terms of the organization of reference information. When an old blog posting on a topic is updated with a new posting, the most recent one can reference the old one, but it does not link to it.

Modification to a Document or Dissemination of Information

Wikis are a superior communication tool when information has to be modified and enhanced as part of a collaborative effort; in contrast, blogs are intended to disseminate information and enable feedback while keeping the original text intact.

Bearing these advantages and disadvantages in mind when you first conceive your digital project will help you choose whether to create a wiki or a blog to enhance your research.

RESEARCH IN ACTION · Didi's story

Didi's course in twentieth-century history required a final research project that meshed with themes from the course readings on some of the problems in recent history related to food and public health. Didi decided she could connect her love of baking to current research around digestive issues caused by wheat consumption. Digestive problems ran in her family, which also fuelled her interest in the subject.

Didi learned that more research needs to be done in order to support people living with conditions that are associated with eating wheat, such as Crohn's disease, colitis, and celiac disease. She also discovered that there was a greater need for information about how gluten affects the digestive system and how this translates into actual gluten-free products such as recipes and specialty goods. These issues became the focus of Didi's Review of Literature. She realized that there were a number of scholarships and publishing opportunities available for students pursuing research at the intersection of history, medicine, and food science.

For her course project, Didi decided to write a 7,000-word essay that she would later submit to a scholarly journal. Since she was not collaborating with other students in the class, she chose to set up a blog reporting on relevant research developments, which she updated regularly. The site she created for her course assignment integrated commentary and critique, historical images, and gluten-free recipes as well as photos of baked goods that she prepared herself.

Didi viewed her course assignment as a first step toward an article and grant application—and perhaps a book sometime in the future. Accordingly, she continued to use the blog format as a way to establish her expertise and build her reputation.

Microblogging

Microblogging refers to social network services that make it possible for Internet users to send short messages in real time to anyone who is interested. The content of microblogging messages ranges from status messages ("I am here" or "This is what I am doing") to links to other Internet sources to commentary on political developments and news events both locally and internationally. There are a number of services, some of which are integrated into platforms such as Facebook and Academia.edu, but probably the best known is Twitter, which went online in 2006.

Twitter

Messages on Twitter, known as tweets, are limited to 140 characters. This restriction has led to the use of abbreviations and extreme condensation of the information communicated. Message senders select from various settings that send their tweet to either a selected group of other Twitter users or, more frequently, to all the other people who have indicated that they want to "follow" an individual user, theme, or development.

Twitter and Hashtags

Certain keywords are marked by Twitter authors and are known as **hashtags**. These keywords—beginning with the metadata tag, #, as in *#technology*—allow you to search for messages related to certain topics. Since the messages are short, the exchange of information can only function within narrow limits.

Uses of Microblogging

A number of scholars use microblogging as a communication tool for the dissemination of academic information. They have found uses for microblogging as a way to quickly disseminate information to a wide audience.

Communication of Conferences and Publications

Microblogging is an effective tool for announcing conferences and other events as well as for drawing attention to publications and Internet sources. Some scholars microblog at conferences or during cultural and social events. The contents of these communications frequently offer commentaries on the organization or substance of presentations even as they are being delivered. As such, microblogging has the ability to function as a backchannel for greater communication and participation.

Scientific Marketing and Communication

Microblogging is also used as a channel for scientific marketing and communication. Organizations and institutions are turning to microblogging to disseminate information quickly and to communicate and promote ideas.

Overall, microblogging is used by individual scholars, by research institutions, and by scholarly journals to circulate brief messages containing information about their work, often accompanied by an indication of where further information can be found online.

Aggregators

Aggregators collect and analyze information from different sources relying on syndication, which we referred to briefly above as RSS, an umbrella term for a variety of XML files that enable the sharing of website content. In fact, RSS can be understood as a web syndication protocol (McKiernan 2004).

Using XML to distribute web content from one website to many other sites, RSS sends a list of headlines and update notices so that new website content is received automatically by those subscribed users who have installed and activated an aggregator.

News Aggregators

A **news aggregator** is "software that periodically reads a set of news sources, in one of several XML-based formats, finds the new bits, and displays them in reverse-chronological order on a single page" (Winer 2002). RSS simply repackages the content as a list that includes, for example, the date of a news story, a summary, and a link. Users can browse the headlines, find a story that interests them, and click through to the actual website. The availability of a web feed for a site is typically indicated by one or more button icons or by a hot-linked word such as *Syndicate* or a phrase such as *Syndicate This Page.* ●))

RSS content is short and fast-loading, so it lends itself readily to use in mobile devices such as smartphones or tablets. After you subscribe to a feed of a news site, blog, or other website, new content from that site is automatically fed to the RSS reader. There are directories such as Bloglines or Technorati that can help you find RSS feeds on topics of specific and personal interest.

RSS feed icon.

Outline Processor Markup Language (OPML)

There is no central repository or library of RSS content—content is distributed all over the Internet. It is possible to share feed lists or a subject-specific feeds list with others by using an Outline Processor Markup Language (**OPML**) file to import complete RSS lists to a news aggregator. You will have to identify sites related to your research and then subscribe.

RSS saves you from having to check sites constantly for updates, especially those that change their content often, such as news sites, stock market reports, and of course, blogs and wikis.

Aggregators and Scholarly Research

Aggregators are useful for keeping up to date with new and changed Internet content, particularly if you are interested in multiple sources of information on many different websites. Web feeds reduce the need to revisit sites for your study so that you can stay apprised of changes or additions. RSS allows you to gather content as it is created and as sites are updated.

Feeds offer a convenient way for you to subscribe only to those sites that are relevant and of interest. Subscribing also provides a service; the more traffic that a site acquires, the more likely it is that content will be refreshed frequently. In addition, the feeds that the aggregators check are virus-free, so you do not have to worry about contaminating your computer if you subscribe to multiple sites.

You can use RSS in conjunction with social bookmarking (see Chapter Four) to create a set of resources accessible via the Internet, to conduct research, to share that research with peers, to track authors, and to document updates.

Advantages and Limitations of RSS

RSS has a number of advantages for both the information-seeking stage of your research and the stage when you are ready to disseminate your work by publishing it online.

Customization

At the search stage, RSS feeds are an efficient way of filtering and customizing the way information is delivered to you.

Efficiency

RSS provides a way to view relevant information in a concise format; it also gives you control over the flow of information and makes it easier for you to share your research with others because it offers such an efficient delivery method.

Increase Traffic to Your Site

At the stage when your digital essay is complete and you would like to share it online, RSS will increase traffic to your website. When it comes time to update your project with new or relevant information, RSS makes it easy to update your work and distribute this information to others. Unfortunately, however, some sites do not have a feed, or the feed expires after a specific time. In addition, there may be copyright issues with some content (especially in the case of libraries, for example).

 FINAL CHECKLIST

- ○ If you are participating in a group project or working as a member of a team, a wiki will likely prove to be a versatile tool for your own tasks and for collaborating with other researchers.

- ○ If you are thinking about building your professional reputation based on special expertise, consider creating a website and starting a blog.

- ○ If you are attending a conference or event and need to let those who are not in attendance know about developments as they take place, or if you would benefit from a tool that allows you

Continued . . .

to distribute short messages that provide news about your work along with notices about where additional information is available online, consider microblogging as a research tool.

○ If you intend to share your thoughts on your research with others on an ongoing basis, consider whether having more than one venue might be appropriate to your needs. For example, you might have a blog, a Twitter account, and a wiki.

○ As you progress with your research, subscribe to websites with RSS feeds in order to keep abreast of developments on key sites you have identified.

Chapter Summary

This chapter presented ways to enhance your research through the use of blogs, microblogs, wikis for collaboration, and aggregators. In the next two chapters, you continue to build your digital vocabulary, acquire greater media competency, and learn about additional tools and techniques you might use for your digital essay.

4

Digital Media in Research

Chapter Outline

Chapter Four and Chapter Five continue with the description and explanation of some of the major digital media tools that began in Chapter Three. Along with the tools that you might want to use for your scholarly essay, we provide examples that can serve as models for your project. Chapter Four focuses on social networks, podcasting, social bookmarking, and folksonomy—all digital tools and techniques that can be used to enhance your scholarship. Keep in mind that there are many examples of these tools—and we are not presenting all of them. Also, some tools will inevitably fall out of favour and will be replaced with newer, more efficient ones. The tools we are listing will help you decide where to begin and how you might use digital techniques.

Social Networks

You probably have experience with online networking sites. **Social networking sites** are web-based services that allow you to construct a public or semi-public profile within a bounded system, to connect and interact with other users with shared interests, and to view your list of connections and those made by others. Studies have shown that those who participate in social network sites are not necessarily "networking" or looking to meet new people; rather, they are primarily communicating with people who are already a part of their extended social network (Boyd and Ellison 2007).

What makes social network sites unique is that they enable you to articulate and make visible your social networks. See the companion website for examples of social networking sites. ◑

Individual Social Networking Sites

Social networking sites allow you to share ideas, activities, events, and interests with others in your network. Begin by creating a profile that provides information about you. Upload pictures to your profile, search for other users with similar interests, and compile and share lists of contacts.

Corporate Social Networking Sites

Not only have individuals been creating networking sites, but a wide variety of organizations have also been creating profiles in recent years to advertise products and services. You can connect with them so that you receive regular status updates about activities at their organization that may help with your scholarly work.

Using Social Networking Sites

You have likely set up your personal network of contacts on a social networking site by sending invitations to other registered members as well as to people outside the network who are not yet participating. User profiles often have a section dedicated to comments from friends and other users.

Social Networking, E-mailing, and Instant Messaging

Social network sites also provide ways for you to interact with other users over the Internet through e-mail and instant messaging. Some networks have additional features such as groups that share common interests or affiliations, live video uploading and streaming, and discussion forums. Carry out a search to see if there are groups already in place that have connected with others with an interest in the information that meshes with various facets of your project.

Real-Time Web (RTW) and Location-Based Services (LBS)

Real-time Web (RTW) and location-based services (LBS) are concepts that are now trending (i.e., showing increased usage) in some social networking sites. Real-time Web allows you to contribute content, which is then published as it is being uploaded.

Location-based services provide information about location and time. For example, LBS allows you to locate the whereabouts of an individual, find the nearest restaurants, or identify other places of interest in an area or neighbourhood. LBS also allows you to track both parcels and vehicles. Facebook's Live Feed streams your activities, comments, or thoughts as soon as they are posted.

You can also embed images and web links within postings. This has contributed to the popularity of social networking sites and has made for a mixture of writing methods.

Social Networking Sites and Public Dialogue

Social networking sites have become a key aspect of web creation. Not only can you map out your social networks but you can carry on a public conversation with your online friends as well. Every interested reader can learn about the intricacies of your daily life. LBS is useful because the technology makes it possible to identify users in your vicinity who are available online and interested in making friends with someone local.

Privacy and Social Networking Sites

Social networking sites have become favourite forums for online interactions. Since forums are relatively easy to access, you need to be aware that the content you post can be viewed by a wide range of people. To protect your privacy, social networks usually have controls that allow you to choose who can view your profile, contact you, or add you to their list of contacts.

Do be aware, however, that privacy on social networking sites can be undermined by many factors. For example, you may disclose so much information that other users are able to identify where you live.

In addition, sites may not take adequate steps to protect user privacy. There are growing concerns about the dangers of giving out too much personal information. These concerns are related to control over your data. For example, information that you alter or remove can still be retained or passed to third parties.

RESEARCH IN ACTION · Octavia's story

A class on Byzantine art that Octavia had to complete for her fine art history degree piqued her interest in jewellery. She learned that many examples of jewellery surviving from the Byzantine and early Islamic periods were immediately evocative to modern sensibilities. As she studied objects that were actually worn by medieval women, Octavia was intrigued by the beauty of these body ornaments and also by the sense of connection she felt with "sisters" from another era.

While Octavia was curating her collection of images of Byzantine jewellery, it struck her that some of the tools and techniques of the period were similar to those she applied in her own practice. She decided to focus her scholarly research on precious metal jewellery and how notions of adornment in the Byzantine era reflected social status. Her Review of Literature was well researched and structured, so it provided her with the categories for analyzing selected items of adornment that would be the focus of her study. She concentrated on three amulets that would have signalled the wealth and status of elite women. After examining the shape, form, and symbols, she identified possible meanings and cultural implications.

As she was engaged in her research, Octavia joined one social networking site for antique jewellery collectors and another that was sponsored by the curator of the Byzantine collection at her local museum. Through these sites, she was able to refine her under-standing of the most significant techniques of construction and her knowledge of the gems and precious metals that were available in medieval culture when these artifacts were created. Her research led her to hone her topic further and to experiment with certain motifs in her own jewellery production.

Ultimately, Octavia set up a website providing descriptions of tools and techniques. It also included her analysis of the symbol-ism found in the amulets that served as the focus of her study. Her website invited people to scan her collection and read her commen-tary. This also led her to the website Etsy, where she registered an account and began selling her jewellery online.

At the same time, if you take suitable precautions, social networking sites can be a source of useful information to draw on when you are creating a digital project.

Social Networking Sites and Research

Social networking sites provide chains of "friends" who can become potential research collaborators. Some sites contain vast stores of multimedia material regarding social movements or groups.

You can create pages that allow you to conduct research online. For example, you might recruit a focus group to watch a video embedded in your page and comment on it. You can put together a profile to disseminate useful information to the public. You might also identify other users with similar academic or scientific interests on social networking sites that target the research community.

Partnering for Collaboration

Research sites offer great potential for partnering in formal scholarly collaborations, especially when all the members of a group are familiar with the technologies (Murthy 2008).

For example, ResearchGate was set up in May 2008, and by early November 2011, had over one million registered members. Members of ResearchGate upload bibliographies that can be shared with others. References to the literature can also be ranked and assessed by users. ◉⟩

Semantic Matching

When you browse a site, you are made aware of relevant new literature and potential contacts on the basis of the profile you provided. This is done via **semantic matching**, which involves connecting information based on correspondences among **ontologies** (systems of classifications arranged in hierarchies that move from general to specific). The matching technique relies on semantic information encoded in ontologies to identify nodes of topics that are related.

Identification of Networks

In addition, networks can be visualized with the aid of interactive graphics. Within the network, you can communicate via direct webmail or through group forums. Webmail and forums are thematically oriented amalgamations of scholars and can be used to exchange sources by way of a shared archive of documents, the circulation of news about upcoming events, or the setting up of shared collections.

Focused Networks

Interactive communities connect individuals based on shared knowledge or experiences. Many provide specialized networking tools and applications that can be accessed via their websites, such as LinkedIn, a professional service that offers a model for how you might disseminate research questions across a community of users who, through their occupations, are interested in the kinds of information you may be pursuing in your research. Look at LinkedIn as an example of the kinds of networks that can be created on the Web, and consider ways to create your own networks focused around your scholarly interests. ◉))

Podcasts

A **podcast** is a series of audio or video media files (such as radio programs or segments, lectures, news, or music) that are typically released episodically and downloaded by web syndication.

A podcast is also a digital media file, either audio or video, that is freely available for download from the Internet. Podcasts are an effective medium for distributing audio and video content for personal use, education, news, entertainment, and business.

The term *podcast* is an amalgam of the word *iPod* (the most popular media player) and *broadcast*, which refers to the traditional methods of receiving information on the television or radio. When British multimedia journalist Ben Hammersley put these two words together in 2004, *podcast* and *podcasting* were born.

Syndication of Podcasts

Podcasting is unique and appealing compared to other methods for accessing media files because its mode of delivery is syndication, which is accomplished through RSS feeds. This gives podcasters the ability to share their content online by subscription.

Podcatcher

The distributor's server contains a listing of audio or video files that are associated with a specific series. *Podcatchers* is the name given to the special client application software that is used to create a podcast and post it on the Internet. These applications can access web feeds, check for updates, and download new files to your computer or to mobile devices such as MP3 players, smartphones, and tablets. Downloading to your system makes it possible to play the podcast offline.

Advantages of Podcasts

Podcasts have many advantages that make them excellent tools for scholarly inquiry:

- Podcasts are personal. They provide an effective way to make contact with other researchers with similar interests. In a digital learning environment, podcasting mimics one-on-one exchanges and gives a virtual sense of what takes place in a traditional seminar or classroom learning environment.
- Podcasts are portable. The portability of podcasts means you can download an offering to your mobile device and listen to it when and where it is convenient.
- Podcasts are available on demand. You can look for past episodes or files with related content and get them right away.
- Podcasts are automatically updated. When you subscribe to a series, you will routinely receive the most recent version without having to follow up yourself.
- Podcasts are effective in bridging physical space in distance learning programs. They make for a more humanized interaction in comparison with e-mail exchanges or discussion board comments.
- Podcasts can be used to provide introductory material before lectures or, more importantly, to record lectures in difficult classes so you can listen to the professor's lecture again and again until you completely understand the material.
- Podcasts can provide additional material to complement lectures.
- Podcasts can supply you with audio tutorial material or exemplary recordings of native speakers for your foreign language courses.

All of these factors are advantages offered by the use of podcasts in scholarly research. ◉))

Podcasting and Education

Even with the increased flexibility in delivering content via podcasting, the technology is still considered in scholarly circles to be more of a supplemental tool than a primary way to distribute information. This situation is likely to change in the years ahead.

The many advantages offered by podcasts will likely mean that they will increasingly become a standard method for delivering course content, conference presentations, and seminars to wider audiences of researchers.

Social Bookmarking

Social bookmarking is a method that allows you to organize, store, manage, and search for bookmarks of resources online. It is not the resources that are shared, but rather the bookmarks that reference those resources. Social bookmarking platforms make it possible to jointly and cooperatively administer, share, and tag bookmarks or on-line literature.

In a social bookmarking system, users who find websites they want to consult again or share will save the links as bookmarks. These bookmarks are usually public, but they can be saved privately, shared with only a few people or groups linked to certain networks, or saved as some combination of public and private.

Those who are allowed access to your information can usually view your bookmarks chronologically, by category or tags, or via a search engine. For your research, this technology can be useful as a way to access consolidated sets of bookmarks from other computers, organize large numbers of bookmarks, and share bookmarks with contacts.

Advantages of Social Bookmarking

Social bookmarking sites that allow you to browse the bookmarks of others—either by examining the bookmarks of friends or by browsing the sites of those who have bookmarked similar sites—are a tremendous advantage in research. Many social bookmarking services encourage you to organize your bookmarks with informal tags instead of the traditional browser-based system of folders, although some services feature categories or folders or a combination of folders and tags. Some also make it possible to view bookmarks associated with a chosen tag. ◗)

Metadata Tags

A **tag** is a keyword and a form of metadata assigned to an image, file, or some other piece of information online. Tags allow information to be relocated in a search enabled by keyword-based classification. Tagging systems encourage you to manually annotate digital objects with keywords and to share these annotations. Best of all, tags can be assigned by anyone.

Tags and Feedback

The instant visibility of a tagged item helps create a feedback mechanism for your ideas. Through feedback, the drawbacks of uncontrolled

A tag cloud.

indexing are less dramatic than in previous systems, and the border between controlled and free indexing is blurred. ◉⟩

Tag Clouds

Tag clouds are visual representations that display each tag in a font size that is proportional to its popularity. Tag clouds do not take into account the meaning of tags or the relationships among them. Relatedness is typically measured with metrics that track the co-occurrence of data. Links to related tags help users find similar items.

Folksonomy

A **folksonomy** is a user-generated taxonomy—as opposed to an authoritative hierarchical taxonomy such as the Library of Congress Subject Headings. A folksonomy is a classification system resulting from personal tagging or social bookmarking of information and objects (anything with a URL) for your own retrieval. Since the tagging is accomplished in a social environment, the folksonomy is typically shared and open to others. "A folksonomy is created from the act of tagging by the person consuming the information" (Vander Wal 2004).

Folksonomy is also referred to as collaborative tagging, social classification, social indexing, and social tagging. In a folksonomy, tags may be reused many times. This can provide information about the popularity of the tags, as well as information about new areas of interest.

Folksonomies and Multiple Users

In fact, folksonomies rely on many users with different perceptions to classify a document rather than relying on one individual cataloguer to set the index terms for an item. Classification terms are therefore relative to each user. "When it comes to searching, what a work means to the searcher is far more important than the author's intention" (Weinberger 2005).

Folksonomies and Libraries

Some libraries allow users to tag catalogue items. User tagging makes it possible for readers to track resources for a research project and make the results available to other scholars. Folksonomies also facilitate different paradigms of navigation based on chance and serendipity. In this "personal tagging," you use your own vocabulary and add meaning, which comes from inferred understanding of the information or object. In this way, social bookmarking or taxonomy allows users to explore two spaces: one for their own bookmarks and one for everyone's bookmarks.

Advantages of Folksonomies

Since folksonomies are multidimensional, you can assign a large number of tags to express a single concept. In addition, you can use your own language, assigning terms that are meaningful to you. More likely than not, these words will be current and will reflect local usage or slang.

Knowledge Creation through Aggregation

Since tags can be shared, they can help create knowledge through aggregation. Collective tagging allows people to contribute to a shared knowledge base, fostering the development of communities around similar interests and viewpoints, which is of significant value in academic research. An item can be tagged with many different terms that in turn can be used to generate an instant collection. Additionally, sub-collections can be assembled by searching for single tags or pairs of tags.

Information about Shared Interests

Another advantage of folksonomies is that they inform others about your areas of interest. The words selected as tags can provide insight into users' information needs and habits.

Ease of Use

Tagging is fast, simple, and straightforward; no formal training in classification or indexing is required. Large-scale, growing folksonomies can bring organization to the tagging process. By evaluating and using existing tags to form useful connections, users can develop unique tagging conventions in the folksonomies through group consensus instead of an externally imposed and possibly dated formal system.

Disadvantages of Folksonomies

In spite of the dynamism of folksonomies, they do have some disadvantages. You should be aware of these issues.

Problematic Tags

The simplicity and ease of tagging is a key feature, but it can result in poorly chosen and applied tags. The creation and application of tags by users who are not experts in information management might lead to problems.

Lack of Hierarchy

Further, the absence of an authority and of a unique and coherent point of view on the domain creates limitations, including lack of hierarchy and an absence of synonym control as well as a dearth of both precision and recall.

The absence of hierarchy might limit the possibility of searching and browsing related information, since tags can be applied at different levels of specificity by different users or even by the same user at different times.

Lack of Connection to a Reference Structure

Folksonomies are not controlled, and tags are not connected to each other by reference structures, which are used in formal systems to link related terms and narrower or broader terms.

Inconsistent Use of Terms

Users may not necessarily be consistent with terms, and different users— or even the same user at different times—might choose different terms for the same concept. For example, the word *shrub* may be used to tag some items, *bush* for others, and *plant* for still others.

Conversely, the same term might be used for different concepts. In many cases, no information about the meaning of a tag is provided (although some systems, such as the social bookmarking service Delicious, do allow tag descriptions).

The choice of tags may also change as new trends evolve; for example, the words *blog, weblog,* and *blogging* will all be used for the same concept. Uncontrolled tagging can result in a mixture of names of things, genres, and formats. It may be difficult to maintain precision when there are no indexing guidelines except those developed by individual users. But certainly many of these problems also plague specialist indexers. For example, the term *video* is sometimes used as a subject heading for an item in a video format as opposed to an item about videos.

Balancing Advantages and Disadvantages of Folksonomies

Problems with user tagging, social bookmarking, and folksonomies are outweighed by the benefits. The technology allows for the richness, currency, relevance, and diversity of terms and collections of resources. The social aspects of tagging folksonomies are perhaps their most important feature.

 FINAL CHECKLIST

○ Use your social networks to share ideas with friends, to identify potential research collaborators, or to connect with sites or forums aligned with your research interests.

○ Check with some of the scholarly social networking sites to see if there are bibliographies or forums that might be of value to your research.

○ Can you use podcasting to create a lecture of your research project? How else might you use podcasting in creative ways?

○ Are there podcasts available that you can integrate into your scholarly study?

○ Determine whether podcasting your professor's lectures will help you master difficult material through repeated listening or viewing.

○ Use social bookmarking sites to link to web pages that will benefit your research.

○ Create a folksonomy for your project.

○ Consider whether web server data logs might provide a viable resource for your research.

Chapter Summary

This chapter explained how social networking sites might be used in scholarly applications. These sites have been established by a wide variety of organizations and special interest groups to promote specific areas of interest. They allow you to set up pages to carry out social research online. Some sites are targeted to the academic community and provide bibliographic research and other significant resources.

Audio or video podcasts are valuable media for distributing files via syndication. Social bookmarking methods make it possible to store, retrieve, organize, and manage bookmarks online as well as tap into the bookmarks of others with similar interests. Folksonomies are collections of tags created by using the user's own keywords.

All of these digital tools and tactics are useful for conducting scholarly research and can be valuable in creating your digital project.

5

Creating with Digital Media Tools

Chapter Outline

Chapter Five continues the description and explanation of some of the major digital media tools from Chapters Three and Four. We describe more of the digital media tools you can use to enhance your academic research, and we present examples that can serve as models for your own scholarship. We concentrate on document sharing, VOIP technologies, digital image collections, digital and streaming video, citation managers, and global positioning system technologies.

Document Sharing

The Internet makes it easy for you to share files and documents with other users. Support for sharing document files is a feature of many web-based collaboration systems. This feature is especially helpful in facilitating collaboration among geographically dispersed researchers.

Additionally, file-sharing sites become a kind of central document repository where the most up-to-date version is always available. As documents are edited, older copies are automatically replaced by newer ones, which are then available and accessible to everyone. When documents are contained in a central repository, access is no longer at the discretion of an individual, department, or division. Work truly becomes a collaborative endeavour that includes everyone in a research community.

In addition, students or researchers can access documents without having to worry about the size of the attachments. Online document sharing makes it possible to send large files without having to split them into smaller sections and then piece them together at the other end. Many websites facilitate the sharing of even very large files of several hundred megabytes. These sites are useful if you want to send whole batches of documents, spreadsheets, databases, presentations, or media files. The process is simple, saves time, and is often free of charge.

Use caution when posting your material. It is important to do some research regarding the privacy and security settings of a document sharing website before uploading your files. ●)

Remote Backup Services

Remote backup services use cloud storage and file synchronization as ways to share folders containing a number of documents for collaborative work—though many were not designed exclusively for this purpose. These web-based file hosting services enable you to house and share files and folders with others across the Internet. Online backup systems such as Dropbox or iCloud, for example, are typically built around a client software program that collects, encrypts, and transfers the data to the server of the remote backup service provider.

Other online backup systems offer similar features but provide different levels of service and types of encryption or target quite specific market segments. High-end **LAN systems** (a local area network that links computers in a smaller area, such as a university) often offer backup services such as Active Directory, client remote control, or open-file backups. Consumer online backup companies frequently have beta software offerings and provide free-trial backup services as well, though many do not offer live support, so you are on your own if you run into difficulties.

Advantages of Online Document Sharing

Online document sharing has a number of advantages for research projects. You can upload your project documents to a central place and invite other students, colleagues, or your professor to view, edit, or comment on them. You can create folders and organize the sections of your project easily, as you do regularly on your personal computer. You can automatically track iterations of uploaded documents and maintain detailed histories of each file.

File-Sharing Protocols

When you are working with a team, there may be multiple copies of a document. You may need to devise protocols to make sure that all the members of your collaborative team upload their edits to the central file so that everyone has access to the most recent version. Sometimes, you might need to have a locking system or a document sharing system.

Version Control Systems

A version control tool, such as the open-source Concurrent Versioning System, can be very useful for complex projects. A locking mechanism stops you from modifying a document while another person is working on it, but then it allows you and other users to access the most recently published version.

Online Services

Online services such as Google Docs offer a free and simple solution for researchers who seek to collaborate, exchange knowledge, and transfer information. Using a web-based document, spreadsheet, or presentation, you obtain data storage from Google Docs for personal and shared files. You can work with others to build projects online at the same time as well as edit each other's work. Open documents are automatically saved to prevent the loss of your data, and a history of your revision is kept automatically.

VoIP Technologies

VOIP or Voice over Internet Protocol is a technology that transmits your voice, image, and instant messages over the Internet instead of through the telephone network. Some commercial providers, such as Google

RESEARCH IN ACTION · Chun Wei's story

Chun Wei was worried about a looming deadline for a group assignment in his urban planning course. He needed an excellent grade in the course in order to improve his chances of gaining admission to a top graduate program in landscape architecture. His group had met and divided the assignment into sections. He had agreed to work with Laurie on the part of the project dealing with urban poverty.

Although Laurie would be away for the next week, she assured Chun Wei they would work on their project every day using Skype and Google Docs. They agreed to have their first session the next day at 6:00 p.m. (Eastern Standard Time). Chun Wei registered at Skype and Google Docs, found Laurie's unique name, and answered her Skype call.

This virtual face-to-face conversation facilitated their collaborative efforts. Chun Wei and Laurie started their session by discussing the research each of them had found. They decided to narrow their focus to the problems of government-assisted housing and to compare and contrast instances of violent crimes in housing projects that crowd low-income people in multiple high-density apartment buildings, as opposed to those that dispersed individual assisted living units throughout established neighbourhoods. While they talked, they used Google Docs to jot down notes, share bibliographies, and organize a Review of Literature. They were able to write together so they were "on the same page."

By the end of their two-hour session, Chun Wei and Laurie had identified a list of housing projects that could serve as possible case studies. They divided the list between them and agreed that each would do more research before their Skype meeting the next day, so they would be prepared to identify one high-density project and one low-density project as the basis for a comparison and contrast analysis.

Chun Wei and Laurie worked together every day. By midweek, they had a solid final draft of their section of the group project. To consolidate their portion of the study with sections of the project undertaken by others, they scheduled a Skype conference call with other members of the group; working simultaneously, the group pulled together all the sections of their project into a cohesive document.

Talk, allow you to connect to any domain on the Internet. Others, such as Skype, are closed so that you can communicate free of charge with anyone in the system. Once you register on Skype, for example, you are assigned a distinctive Skype Name that is listed in their "phone book." You can then communicate with other registered users individually or via conference calls. The system also preserves a record of your chat history and allows you to edit previous messages.

Digital Image Collections

A digital image is a two-dimensional image that is represented numerically. Digital images are composed of **pixels**, short for picture elements, the smallest individual unit in an image. Each pixel represents the colour (for colour images) or grey level (for black and white images) at a single point in the picture.

A digital image is a rectangular array of pixels sometimes called a **bitmap**. Typically, the pixels are stored in a computer's memory as a **raster image** or **raster map**, a two-dimensional array of small integers. These values are often transmitted or stored in a compressed form.

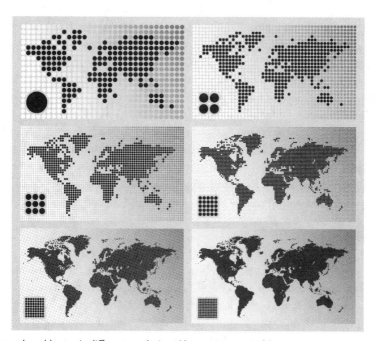

Dotted world maps in different resolutions (dots represent pixels).

Keywords and the Digital Image Search

Note that online digital image searching relies on words to locate results, and so it is sometimes hard to find images if they are not named to reflect their content. This is why it is a good idea to use different keywords when you carry out a search on digital image collections. ◉))

University Library Image Collections

Image databases available through university libraries are generally licensed for educational use. A university's faculty, staff, and students do not need additional permission to use the images in classroom instruction or related educational activities, including presentations and student assignments.

Online Image Collections

Unlike the databases available through university libraries, image collections freely viewable on the Web are not licensed for educational use. Although many online images are available free of charge and without permission for non-commercial use, others require permission from the owner before you can use them. So prior to choosing an image for your work, read the usage rights for the collection or individual image and, if necessary, seek the copyright owner's permission to use the picture.

There are a number of useful resources for conducting an image search. The following are just a few of the digital image tools available for researchers today, and newer ones are emerging regularly.

Google, Yahoo, and Exalead

Google's Advanced Image Search allows you to limit your search by size, colour, and other parameters. Yahoo Image Search offers image searching capabilities similar to Google's, but across a different collection of images; compared to other search engines, Yahoo gives a higher priority to images from Flickr. Exalead Image Search is another advanced image search engine.

Behold Image

The Behold search engine identifies high-quality Flickr images and searches for images at the level of the pixel. Whereas standard image search engines such as Flickr and Google search through images using only image tags and filenames, Behold uses both aesthetic and technical quality indicators to search pixel patterns available online. Many of these images may be used free of charge; others have some restrictions.

The Digital Images Collections Wiki

The Digital Images Collections Wiki is a collection of free-use and fair-use digital images. The main goal of this site is to provide an image-gathering tool for art history students and faculty. The tool was developed using the wiki format so that users can continue to add their own bookmarked fair-use galleries and evolve the resource on an ongoing basis.

The wiki links to images from other websites. Since the site does not host any of the actual images, the size and quality will differ from site to site.

Instagram

Instagram is a mobile social networking application that allows users to post and share photos. Unlike other social networks, Instagram is focused solely on image creation and sharing. It has particular features that allow you to use your mobile phone to edit, filter, and post photos, as well as to follow other users and create networks of online friends. Since the focus is on mobility, it is a good tool for those who need a way to collaborate on the go.

Pinterest

Pinterest is a content-sharing service that makes it possible for members to "pin" images, videos, and other objects to a "pinboard." The tool allows users to organize images from web searches into collections and then add tags and information. The kind and quality of the board depends on the user's search skills and the number of people who participate.

Pinterest is a valuable tool for searching for images by interest. Researchers can also curate their own collection of images for sharing, building collaborative projects, and learning about topics from a visual point of view. You can search for images by "pinners," "pins," and "boards." For example, a "do-it-yourself" board will produce a large number of images with instructions for creative projects. The more detailed the search, the greater the likelihood that you will find images related to your project.

JSTOR

JSTOR (short for Journal Storage) is an online system for archiving academic journals that is available through universities, libraries, and other scholarly institutions. JSTOR's image database is a rich and valuable resource. Use your library card (or university username and password) to search online not only for complete texts of back issues of peer-reviewed journals but also for images. You can also search for captions to images. If you perform a search and then click on the "Images in JSTOR" tab, the results will be limited to images only.

ARTstor

ARTstor is a digital repository of images and related data focused on the work of the arts and education community. To find images in the ARTstor database, perform a search and then further limit the search to images only by clicking on the "Images in ARTstor" tab at the top of the results list.

Digital and Streaming Video

Digital video is audiovisual material in a binary form. Information is presented as a sequence of digital data rather than as a continuous signal (the way analog information is presented). Streaming video is content that is sent in compressed form over the Internet and then displayed by the viewer in real time.

Digital Video and Analytic Software

Digital video consists of discrete units of data placed close together so that the human eye perceives them as flowing continuously. Digital video technology can incorporate analytical software for intelligent video, which enables video searches, object tracking, and intrusion detection.

To take advantage of digital video, you need a player. Players can be integral parts of browsers or downloaded from a software maker's website. Since the data is in compressed form, you need to expand the information to send visual data to the display and audio data to the speakers.

Streaming Video Content

With streaming video or streaming media, you do not have to wait to download a file in order to play it. The media is sent in a continuous stream of data and plays as it arrives.

Video stream servers provide video content in a generic form, using protocols other than http (such as rtps, rtmp, or rtp) so that anyone can access them.

The video is typically streamed from pre-recorded video files. It can also be distributed as part of a live broadcast feed. In a live broadcast, the signal is converted into a compressed digital signal and transmitted from a special web server that is capable of **multicasting**, or sending the same file to multiple users at the same time.

As fast Internet connections became commonplace (at least in developed countries), many websites began delivering programs or movies online. Recent developments in hard drive capability and flash memory recording make it possible to easily embed videos in blogs, websites, and other Internet forums.

YouTube

Perhaps the most well-known streaming video site is YouTube. You no doubt know that YouTube is a website that allows you to watch videos as well as post your own online—so they can be seen around the globe. The site makes it possible for you to create your own video content, attach a title and keywords so others can easily find your work, and post your production online.

YouTube offers a number of choices in content such as educational lectures, scholarly presentations, tutorials, class projects, current event items, hobby and special interest pieces, comedy routines, and recipes.

The site has three main features. The first is **video embedding**, which allows you to insert YouTube video clips into your blog or website. The second is the option of public or private videos, which offers you an opportunity either to broadcast your videos publicly or to keep them private so that they can only be accessed by your friends or fellow students. The third feature is subscriptions; these make it possible for you to keep track of your favourite videos and users on the site. Remember, the better the lighting and sound recording, the better the video. Especially if you are creating a piece for academic credit, you will want to make certain that your video is as close to professional quality as you can make it. ◉

Citation Managers

Citation managers, also called bibliographic software, citation software, or reference managers, can be used to import citations from your favourite databases and websites, build and organize bibliographies, format citations for papers, take notes on articles and file them in your collection of citations, and save and organize your PDFs, screenshots, graphs, images, and other files for research.

RefWorks, EndNote, and Zotero are the most popular and powerful citation managers currently being promoted and supported by academic library websites (Hensley 2011). RefWorks and EndNote both allow you to import thousands of citations into your own database and format them into any citation style. They also feature "cite as you write" capability.

Records cannot be transferred from one program to another, so you are limited to choosing only one citation manager. The most important consideration in selecting the software is to find the one that is used by the majority of your colleagues so that you will avoid problems when you need to share your research.

A warning, however: you will need to double-check every entry against your style guide. Bibliographies created with these programs produce so many anomalies and inconsistencies in capitalization and punctuation that the product can only be considered a rough version that must be revised and refined by hand. Many professors are annoyed when they see a bibliography created by a citation manager that the student has not double-checked—and they grade the assignment accordingly.

RefWorks

RefWorks is web-based and compatible on all platforms. Most database vendors have adapted their interfaces to export references relatively easily into RefWorks. You can import references from library catalogues, other citation managers, RSS feeds, and websites as well.

Since RefWorks added an attachment feature, you can upload 100 MB of a variety of file types (although an administrator can increase this limit to 5 GB). However, you do need access to the Internet to use the functionality of the RefWorks database of citations. Be aware as well that the interface of each article database uses a different process for exporting references.

EndNote

The EndNote program is most heavily used in the sciences. It is compatible with Windows and Mac and is accessible offline. Online access, available through EndNote Web, is limited to 10,000 records.

EndNote allows you to search across the full text of PDFs and extract metadata from PDFs. In addition, records can be viewed side by side, compared, and edited. Unfortunately, file attachments are not accessible from EndNote, and there are no cloud storage options, so you need to find your own solution for backing up your database.

Zotero

Zotero is a free-of-charge extension of the Firefox browser that allows automatic synchronization across multiple computers and provides back-up space on its servers. Zotero is relatively intuitive and uses drag-and-drop technology. Importing references is not as complicated as it is in RefWorks and EndNote. You simply click on the Zotero item image in Firefox's location bar, and the citation information is added to your library.

Zotero also has a "cite as you write" application that works in Microsoft Word, MacWord, and OpenOffice. Unlike RefWorks and EndNote, Zotero also works with Google Docs.

Since data is saved in your Firefox browser, storage space is limited to 100 MB of free cloud-based storage. You have to pay for additional data access. So keep in mind that Zotero can be limiting if you are working with a high volume of citations.

Mendeley

Mendeley is citation management software that "promotes collaborative work and weaves itself into the research process rather than simply organizing citations" (Hensley 2011). The Mendeley dashboard combines desktop and web-based applications and is compatible across platforms.

The system is intuitive to learn and features drag-and-drop technology. There is a "cite this document" feature that allows users to copy and paste a citation for a single item using the major citation styles. Another valuable feature of Mendeley is its PDF management capability that includes importation of PDF metadata, automatic naming and filing of documents, opening of multiple PDFs, and the ability to highlight, to annotate within the application, and to mark papers as read or unread. ●))

Yet another feature is that it allows a research team to collaboratively annotate and share notes. The notes can be limited to the group or opened to the public. Viewing the work of other teams makes it possible to observe research trends (Hensley 2011).

Sente

Sente is a scholarly reference manager for Mac OS X users; it is also available as a mobile app. Sente can search and retrieve references from sources such as PubMed or Thomson Reuters (ISI) Web, and it can also be used to manage PDF files. It can create bibliographies in APA, Chicago, MLA, and other formats.

It works with word processing software such as Microsoft Word, Apple's Pages, Mellel, Nisus Writer, and OpenOffice. ●))

The Importance of Citation Managers

Citation management software is an important means for building your research agenda. You should be fluent with at least one citation manager in order to keep track of your bibliographic searches. Note, however, that new citation software will become available and the software we have listed will be updated as glitches are discovered and new features added.

Global Positioning System (GPS) Technologies

Global positioning system (GPS) technologies are made possible by satellites orbiting the earth that transmit information about geographic location and time.

Location-Based Services (LBS)

Location-based services (LBS) integrate geographic location with the user's own context (city, town, college campus) to deliver precise information about buildings, restaurants, health services, or recreational opportunities at a certain place in real time. With the advent and spread of smartphones, tablets, and other mobile devices, major opportunities for collecting and using LBS data for scholarship have become available.

Geotagging

Geotagging involves adding geographical identification metadata to various types of digital media such as photos, videos, podcasts, websites, SMS messages, blog entries, or social network posts. The data typically consists of latitude and longitude coordinates, but it can also include altitude, accuracy data, and place names.

There is no single standard for geotagging; a number of techniques are available for adding geographical identification metadata to an information resource. One convention, established by Geobloggers and increasingly used by other sites such as Flickr and Delicious, enables content to be found via a location search.

Geotagging can help you find a range of location-specific information. For example, it is possible to find images taken near a specific location by entering latitude and longitude coordinates into an image search engine. Geotagging-enabled information services can also be used to find local news or websites that pertain to both commercial and personal enterprises. ◉⟩

Geocoding

Geocoding involves taking geographic identifiers, such as a street address or postal code, and finding associated geographic coordinates (or vice versa for reverse geocoding). This process can be used together with geotagging to provide alternative search techniques.

Examples of online map services include Google Maps, Yahoo Maps, MapQuest, Microsoft TerraServer, and Google Earth. These services are useful for finding driving directions, and they also allow you to obtain

RESEARCH IN ACTION · Joslyn's story

Joslyn had a digital assignment for her geography class. She recalled going on a campus tour and learning about the different points of interest at her university. She developed a bibliography focusing on public tours and how they represent an institution's point of view. She then wrote a Review of Literature that described how different institutions understand their space and geography.

Joslyn decided to create a map that highlighted points of interest and provided additional data that was not part of the regular campus tour. This tour highlighted important works of art found on campus, the best places to eat, and places for quiet study. Each point of interest included metadata and other information useful for visitors and new students. Joslyn's map demonstrated how tours in general could be mapped in ways that highlight individual experiences rather than institutional expectations.

satellite pictures, topographical images, three-dimensional images, and angled aerial photography.

Some of the common features of these online map services include geotagging, mapping, geocoding, and points of interest (POI) searching. Geotagging map services provide tools you can use to add map annotations using either shapes or text. Mapping is very useful for displaying georeferenced data and for producing aesthetically pleasing data visualizations.

A number of map services provide a geocoding engine that calculates a location's latitude and longitude coordinates, including street addresses and intersections, street blocks, and postal codes. Many map services have a detailed database of businesses and landmarks that you can search either by category or by name. ◉)

Digital Technologies and Scholarship

In using technology in your academic work, you should look at digital tools as part of a larger "information ecology." The idea is to use technology in order to expand the dimensions of the more traditional learning and research assignments.

Services such as Twitter and blogs are well suited to sharing information. Some will appeal to you more than others, based on your personal learning and scholarship style. Finding the right tools for you and your project, and applying them in novel ways, will allow you to be a more efficient and productive scholar.

Digital media tools make it possible for you to join together with other scholars and to configure and personalize systems according to your needs, skills, and talents. For example, your blog can open access to other information (such as Delicious bookmarks or Twitter tweets of those with similar interests) and facilitate communication—interested others can contact you via Facebook.

Always be mindful when posting material on the Internet that sharing certain opinions or experiences can come back to haunt you years later when they are read by potential employers or colleagues.

 FINAL CHECKLIST

○ Think about your project in relation to the tools and techniques available to you for researching, writing, and creating your digital essay.

○ Consider various combinations of tools to enhance your scholarship.

○ Set up a Dropbox account or open an online backup system for cloud storage and document sharing.

○ Set up a Skype account and practise using virtual face-to-face conversations.

○ Curate a collection of digital images using such programs as Flickr, Pinterest, or Instagram.

○ Learn how to upload video to YouTube or other online streaming programs.

○ Choose a citation manager and begin inputting your bibliographic data.

○ Apply geotagging metadata to sites that interest you.

Chapter Summary

This chapter presented the third of three sections of this book that focus on the digital tools available to enrich your scholarly research. To help you select the right tools for your particular project, we discussed document sharing, VoIP technologies, digital image collections, digital and streaming video, citation managers, and global positioning system technologies.

6

The Proposal

Chapter Outline

Chapter Six describes and explains how to create an effective formal proposal. What makes a quality document? We provide a condensed outline of the elements that go into a proposal and explain how to integrate them into a cohesive work. We also describe how to summarize the research you have undertaken to arrive at an achievable project and how to set forth a clear map of the work you will carry out in future. A proposal functions as a contract with your instructor and university and as a guide to the work you need to do to successfully complete your project. Our checklist helps you organize the various components of the proposal.

Creating a Quality Proposal for a Digital Project

Outstanding project proposals respond directly to the aims and objectives for the assignment. They use clear and concise language to describe projects that are aligned with the goals of the research expected by the professor or thesis committee. Good project proposals describe research that is achievable given the time and resources available. They also provide evidence of thorough research, careful documentation, and a full understanding of relevant methods.

Your proposal should identify a problem, ask a question, and bring two or more bodies of research together in a literature review and a bibliography that demonstrate your skills in library and Internet research. You show that you possess these skills in your proposal by analyzing a vast amount of information and then organizing, structuring, and synthesizing previous scholarship so that the argument for your study emerges from the research. The proposal also considers the range of digital media available, selects the proper tools, incorporates them into the methodology, and explains how the methods will be employed to conduct the rest of the study.

The Purpose of a Proposal

The purpose of the proposal is to present the following information:

- provide background and present an overview of the problem;
- ask one or more research questions;
- describe the current state of knowledge regarding the problem and the debates in a discipline;
- situate your study within this ongoing dialogue; and
- describe the methods and technologies you will be using to carry out the work you propose.

In other words, you are asking your instructor for approval to do the following:

- continue researching your topic of interest;
- write a larger research paper, which includes an Introduction, Review of Literature, Methodology, Analysis or Body of the study, Results or Findings, Conclusion, Endnotes, Bibliography, and Appendix/es; and
- create a digital media product related to the research study.

The Basic Proposal Format

Proposals must anticipate the entire project. A condensed description of the parts of a proposal is presented in this chapter.

Since creating a proposal involves looking ahead to work that will be carried out in the future, we offer advice to help you determine how to select the best ideas and tools. Be aware that the format we describe below is the basic format for a research proposal and that innumerable variations on this format are possible. You should adapt the format to suit the needs of your project. We offer some suggested word counts and page parameters for a hypothetical 7,000 word digital essay (about 20 to 25 print pages), which is a fairly standard length for many published journal articles. Proposals for theses and dissertations are typically about this length.

Additionally, the proposal serves as the preliminary draft of the first one-third to one-half of the final essay. In upcoming chapters, we present a more detailed account of the sections common to both the proposal and the final project.

Proposals typically have the following major sections:

- Introduction;
- Review of Literature;
- Methodology and Digital Media;
- Endnotes or Footnotes; and
- Bibliography. ◉

Customizing the Basic Format

How you set out the information in your document, including the order of the components, should be negotiated with your course instructor. The basic formula describes the typical minimal requirements a proposal needs to fulfill in order to receive approval to carry out the rest of your research. You are demonstrating that you have taken into account the ground covered by previous scholarship and that you can point to possible areas that require further inquiry. Your goal should be to accomplish the following:

- demonstrate critical thinking about your subject;
- contextualize the major theoretical constructs within one or more disciplines and evaluate them;
- show how you have conducted thorough library and Internet searches;

- critique previous methods and propose an approach for your research that corrects problems with other approaches you have identified through the research;
- show that you can write a clear narrative of the debates taking place in your subject area, weigh evidence, and critically engage with the current understandings of the problem;
- suggest an innovative digital undertaking; and
- document your thinking.

Proposed Title for Your Project

From the beginning, give your study a working title. Titles are important in that they arouse the curiosity of readers and let them know what the work is about. Academic titles are typically divided into two parts separated by a colon. Before the colon is a more poetic or idiomatic title; what comes after the colon is a more straightforward and precise description of the research. Consider the following:

> Under the Gun: Journalism, Narrative, and the Literary Persona of
>   Hunter S. Thompson in *Fear and Loathing in Las Vegas*
> Black and White: Image, Text, and Sound in the Adaptation from Graphic
>   Novel to Film in Marjane Satrapi's *Persepolis*
> Lost in Translation: A Digital Text Analysis of Wim Wenders's *Wings of
>   Desire* and Brad Silberling's *City of Angels*

As these examples make clear, if you are focusing on a case study or a particular object, event, or work of literature, you should identify them in the section of the title that follows the colon.

A great title captures attention; makes explicit the subject of inquiry; describes the analysis; indicates the specific example/s, case studies, texts, or elements that will serve as the focus of inquiry; and points to the proposed digital technologies and techniques.

General Considerations

Disciplinary conventions differ and every project is unique. Still, excellent projects typically have all or most of the basic elements but alter the proportions. For example, thematic studies in English, French, or Spanish literature may not call for a hypothesis but will still retain the other elements. Certain scientific fields require a more extensive discussion of the methodology relative to arts and humanities disciplines. Be aware of your disciplinary conventions and customize the format for your topic and field. As a rough guide, we have included sample sizes and lengths for each element.

Active or Passive Voice?

Remember that some disciplines use the passive voice for scholarly narratives:

> The following aspects were studied . . .

Other fields regularly use the active voice:

> I studied the following aspects . . .

Interdisciplinary research typically invites a first-person account as in the example above that makes use of the active voice.

Having a clear grasp of the style of voice for your research paper is a basic question to answer as you begin drafting a proposal. If you have gathered a number of model papers in your field, and the majority use the passive voice, then this is a good indication that you should do so as well. If you are unsure about which voice you should adopt, then double-check with your instructor.

The Introduction

The first major component of your proposal is the Introduction. In a senior undergraduate or graduate proposal of about 7,000 words or 20 to 25 printed pages, introductions are generally 500 to 1,000 words or two to four printed pages long. There are ten basic elements in many introductions:

- problem;
- question;
- hypothesi;s
- thesis statement;
- statement of significance;
- purpose;
- scope and limitations;

- definitions;
- assumptions; and
- outline of steps to the argument.

Problem

Begin with a one-paragraph summary of the problem. This paragraph often establishes the big picture and moves from general to specific. In other words, you might start with a statement that describes the overall problem. The following example illustrates this approach:

> We are living at a time of revolutionary transformation in communication media.

Following the opening sentence, offer a few more statements that go more deeply into the issues, or recount the main facts and background information crucial to understanding the problem in context:

> The convergence of photography, audio and video recording, the cellular telephone, and the computer, the Internet, e-mail, and fax, has made information exchange instantaneous. Communication practices are reconfiguring around material shifts in infrastructures, altering institutions, the economy, society, and culture.

Next, narrow the lens to focus on a controversy, debate, or gap in the literature:

> Some researchers maintain that innovative technologies [K] are key to a prosperous future (de Kerckhove 2000; Gaffield 2013; Levy 2001). Others warn of . . . (Taylor 2013; Burrus 2012). While issues related to K, namely, L, M, and N, have been the subject of heated debate in the literature, the discussion has concentrated on X, Y, Z. Q has received less attention.

Notice that references in parenthetical citations are grouped according to the stance of the particular scholars in the debate.

Next, you may want to narrow the lens of your inquiry to the specific subjects, events, and/or phenomena that you will analyze in the Analysis or Body section of your study:

> The issues surrounding Q are compelling and urgent. In particular, scholars are puzzled over A.

The opening statements should be quite general. Each additional statement should become increasingly specific, leading to a very particular subject that points to a clear and precise research question.

Research Question

Following the first or second paragraph, write one to three sentences that ask up to three focused, clearly formulated research questions. The questions should delimit the area that you will be concentrating on in your inquiry and set the stage for the entire study. For example, research questions are often stated in terms of relationships:

> How might the relationships between K and Q transform culture?

In addition, questions that begin with *how* typically invite stronger explanations rather than simple descriptions.

Hypothesis

The hypothesis typically follows the research question and indicates what you expect to find as a result of the research and why. The hypothesis is generally one to three sentences long. A hypothesis predicts outcomes and formulates the thesis in a testable way. In other words, it explains how you will go about testing the claims in the thesis statement. If you claim that "advances in classroom technology have played a major role in improving learning in undergraduate education," what evidence will you cite to back up that claim?

A hypothesis predicts results. Consider the following:

> The hypothesis in this study is that the blue liquid will turn purple when red liquid is added.

This sentence can sometimes be formulated as a null hypothesis:

> It is not the case that blue liquid will turn purple when red liquid is added.

Ultimately, you may not use the hypothesis in your final essay, but it can serve as a placeholder for the thesis statement in the early stages of research before you have had an opportunity to decide on your argument. After you work out an argument, you may want to remove the hypothesis from your Introduction.

RESEARCH IN ACTION · Ted's story

Ted's project proposal for his public health course was on innovations in medical technology. Many of the studies in the literature concentrated on the benefits of medical advances. Yet Ted also found a number of reports documenting harmful effects. He noted that these problems were seldom subjected to the same level of analysis as the beneficial effects. Ted decided that this was an area in the literature that could provide a niche for his study.

Moving from general to specific in the Introduction section of his proposal, Ted began by drawing attention to the big picture as background to his problem. He wrote the following opening sentence:

> Technological advances in medicine and biology raise profound ethical questions about the nature and potential of human beings.

Having pointed to the overall area for his study, Ted narrowed the discussion to some specific examples:

> Bioengineering, pharmacology, cloning, genetic engineering, enhancement technologies, and other body and brain modifications hold the possibility of changing the species (Parens 1998).

Ted then referred to a critical debate in the literature by identifying opposing views:

> While many people point to the benefits of technology, anti-technology activists and critical social theorists of science and technology are deeply concerned that interfering with nature will cause irreparable harm (Young 2000, 407–10).

Ted went on to identify a need that is a point of agreement among everyone involved in the debate, which functioned as a preliminary statement of significance:

> Finding a way to work through the moral issues and ethical dilemmas presented by new technologies has been identified as a critical priority by parties on all sides of this debate.

Ted highlighted the crux of the problem:

> The problem is particularly pressing because the bioethical principles of autonomy, beneficence, non-maleficence, and justice (see Beauchamp and Childress 2009) have proven to be an overly simplistic framework for dealing with complex ethical issues emerging at the intersection of technology and medicine (Keenan 1999, 104–20).

Ted narrowed the discussion to a specific instance of the problem:

> Scholars have identified the principle of autonomy as particularly problematic (Takala 2001, 72–7).

Then he stated the research question:

> Given the complexity of many ethical dilemmas in biomedical technology today, it is fair to ask, Is the principle of autonomy an adequate frame for ethical decision-making in biology and medicine?

Ted was on his way to gaining approval for his research study.

Alternatively, the hypothesis can remain in the final essay to contrast with the thesis statement. It might be advantageous for you to explain the results you expected going in to the study as opposed to the results you actually obtained. In a thesis on Canadian fictional literature, for example, it may be helpful to have a hypothesis in case you do not find the result you expected:

> The hypothesis is that in a country with a significant immigrant population such as Canada, "a return to the homeland" will be a common theme in works of fiction.

If you survey the literature and do not find this theme very often, you would have to start over and reformulate the entire argument. However, if you have a hypothesis, you simply state that you did not find the theme and try to explain why. The value of disconfirming the hypothesis is that others will know to avoid following the same route.

Thesis Statement

The thesis statement sets forth the argument and related claims and is therefore the single most important component of the proposal. The thesis statement is typically one to three sentences. Good thesis statements get right to the point:

> The thesis in this study is . . .
> This study argues . . .
> I argue . . .

All thesis statements entail one or more claims. State these claims up front:

> This study demonstrates . . .
> Evidence indicates that . . .
> I assert . . .

Thesis statements may also include some of the evidence that gives warrant (or supports) the claims:

> I argue that the health issues are more serious than has previously been supposed. My survey showed that fully one-third of the population . . .

Statement of Significance

The explanation of the significance of the study is important in all proposals and can be stated in anywhere from a few sentences up to a few
paragraphs. What is at stake? Why should your reader—or indeed anyone—care? Who is affected? What are the implications? What happens
if nothing is done? How is the specific case relevant and significant as
an instance of wider issues?

It is essential to let your readers know why your research is worthwhile. If you are not clear about why your research is important, no one
else will be either. If your study is not important, why should readers
bother to read further? What reasons can you offer that will persuade
them that your work has major ramifications?

Purpose

Mention the aim, objective, goal, or purpose of the study in one or two
sentences. What does the research seek to achieve? What are your two
or three main objectives in carrying out the investigation? Do you have
one or two substantial goals for your project? What are your reasons for
organizing the research in the way that you have?

Keep in mind that undergraduate and master's level research projects
rarely have the capacity to *prove* anything. Instead, you should *demonstrate, illustrate, examine, analyze,* and *show*. In other words, you will
want to demonstrate that there are compelling reasons for accepting
your argument, even though it is unlikely that you will be able to prove
your case.

Statement of Scope and Limitations

The statement of scope and limitations puts borders around your
study. The statement is generally two or three sentences long. The scope
explains the full parameters of the project. The limitations make explicit
what is not included. Here are some examples:

> Focusing on the Book of Genesis in the Old Testament, only the chapters
> concerning the Fall and the Flood will be considered.
>
> This study centres on Margaret Atwood's *The Handmaid's Tale*, though
> several passages from Atwood's other novels will be briefly mentioned.
>
> The small sample size and absence of a control group in this qualitative
> research study may have skewed the results.

Limitations also explain why the study might be in error:

> Further testing will be required in order to confirm these results.

Preliminary Definitions

Many but not all studies require that you define a set of terms. Preliminary definitions are generally five or six sentences, if necessary. If your research relies on one or more words as the focus of investigation such as "the system and doctrine in Plato's dialogues" or "euphemisms for death in Holocaust narratives," you may want to specify with precision how you will be using *system* or *euphemisms*.

In an academic study, citing a dictionary definition is seldom acceptable. Nor is it satisfactory to simply quote one author's definition unless it has become standard in the field or you are critiquing it. Create your own unique definition by melding versions offered by several authors, and cite their work.

Assumptions

Make overt reference to any assumptions you have made in the investigation. The reason you want to make your assumptions clear is that they may not be accurate. While some ideas may be taken for granted even by leading scholars in a discipline, further research may reveal them as faulty—for example, you should question "women are the weaker sex" or "it was assumed that the sample surveys from residents earning minimum wage at the Gateway Trailer Park were representative of low-income and working poor families."

Outline of Argument

At the end of the Introduction, describe the steps to the argument in one or two paragraphs. By this, we do not mean listing the components of the essay as we have listed the names for the various components described above. Rather, indicate the ordering of the information you will be presenting in your essay so as to lead readers to accept your argument:

> In the first section of this study, I present the research on carbon dating of skeletal remains. . . . In the second section, I present results from carbon dating analysis of the C6D1442 remains. . . . Finally, I explain why previous studies have underestimated the age of . . .

The purpose of this section of the study is to provide readers with an advance picture of the territory you will be covering. This advance warning lets them know how you have shaped your argument, provides a sense of the overall project, and explains how evidence will be presented so as to support the claims made in the thesis statement. The outline of the steps to the argument should indicate the conclusions reached at the end of each section as well as how they come together to create a cohesive study.

Review of Literature

The Review of Literature is the second major section of the proposal and is generally three to six pages in length. It is basically a description and critique of what the academic literature—the books, chapters, articles, journals, and other most often cited sources—reveals about the subject you are investigating. It is an inquiry and critique of one or more subject areas. .

The literature review provides the entire framework for your research and critically examines the methods, tools, and criteria you will need in order to perform the analysis and interpretation of the study. Many students are relatively new researchers in their chosen subject areas before they start reading. The idea of the literature review is to demonstrate to your readers that you have acquired a good working knowledge of the research that is available on your topic so that you are prepared to carry out the rest of the investigation you propose.

In addition to expanding your knowledge and understanding of the topic, writing a literature review helps you gain and demonstrate skills in two areas: information-seeking and critical appraisal. The Review of Literature shows that you are able to scan the literature efficiently, using both manual and computerized methods, and that you can identify a set of useful articles and books. It also demonstrates that you have the ability to apply principles of analysis to identify relevant studies, weigh the evidence offered, evaluate strengths and weaknesses, and assess their value relative to your project.

Anatomy of the Review of Literature

A literature review typically brings together two to three different bodies of literature or fields of inquiry. A discussion and evaluation of appropriate digital tools may be included in one of these sections.

Accordingly, this part of the proposal frequently begins with an introduction that is followed by two or three linked sections, each one a kind of mini-essay explaining a body of literature that you consulted in order to understand the problem or answer the research question. Each of the sections of the review evaluates evidence from that body of literature relative to the question, hypothesis, thesis, methods, and tools you are considering for your study. Following the sections dealing with different bodies of literature, there should be one or more paragraphs bringing these fields of inquiry together and describing the results or findings of the investigation.

For the proposal, the Review of Literature is a draft that will likely be refined, revised, and tightened for the final project.

Introduction to the Review of Literature

The Review of Literature opens with an introductory paragraph describing the areas of research that you are drawing upon to respond to the question, to test hypotheses, and to support your claims. An introduction also explains not only which bodies of literature you have examined but also why you have chosen these particular fields. You need to explain the reasoning that led you to select these bodies of literature and why they are relevant to your study. Why have you chosen this ordering? Have you arranged them in accordance with their importance to your project or on the basis of some other principle?

Sections of the Review of Literature

The sections that follow the introduction to the literature review set forth the research literature and assess the arguments, claims, assumptions, views, and positions of the authors. Sometimes the literature review follows a chronological or historical sequence. More often it (1) abstracts main principles, issues, ideas, and methods; (2) groups authors around various positions, views, or methods; and (3) assesses or weighs the evidence those authors present. A good literature review almost never moves from author to author or book to book.

Keep in mind that every mini-essay or section of the literature review must flow into the subsequent paragraph or section through the effective use of transition statements.

Purpose of the Review of Literature

The aim of the Review of Literature is to set forth the "state of the art" concerning current knowledge about a particular problem and question, uncover gaps in the literature, identify problems or controversies, expose unquestioned assumptions, and highlight different methods and digital tools so as to situate a research study in an ongoing dialogue. A related aim is to find a foothold for your work that shows how your study builds upon existing knowledge even as it goes on to make an original contribution. Above all, the literature review does more than simply describe previous research—it looks at the quality of the arguments and evidence, and it weighs, assesses, and critiques them.

The Review of Literature ends with a brief summary of the salient points of the literature. This summary highlights the main themes, issues, ideas, questions, or approaches that will govern the Analysis or Body portion of the project. In this way, a literature review creates the major devices, tools, criteria, or "instruments" that will be applied to your own inquiry and interpretation in subsequent sections of the study.

Methodology and Digital Tools and Techniques

The third major section of the proposal is the Methodology, which is generally 250 to 1,000 words or one or more print pages in length. This section includes a digital tools and techniques subsection, which describes the research method/s to be applied to the topic and how digital media fit into the research. In a few short paragraphs, this section justifies the approach that will be taken in the study in light of the methods or issues discussed in the Review of Literature. Procedures and protocols are often outlined.

Digital Tools

As part of the Methodology section, you need to provide a short description of the digital project and its relationship to the research agenda. This description is typically one to three paragraphs. Survey the digital media tools that are relevant to your research and explain why you have chosen to use them for your digital essay.

Timeline

If the assignment requires a timeline, indicate in point form a series of dates for the components of the final project so that your instructors know that you have engaged in serious planning. The timeline is usually one page in length.

Bibliography

The fourth major component of the proposal is the Bibliography. A refined and perfected bibliography is a key element of the proposal. It should include the sources cited in the proposal plus any works that you may be drawing upon in the full-length study. The bibliography is what demonstrates the thoroughness of your research skills. The level of care you have taken in making sure that all the entries are correctly and consistently formatted is a sign of the effort you have taken with the entire proposal. The bibliography should be a minimum of four pages but is often much longer.

The bibliography should be meticulously assembled using the style guide relied on most often by senior scholars in your discipline, such as the guides published by the Modern Languages Association (MLA), the American Psychological Association (APA), and the University of Chicago. The bibliography should be comprehensive, accurate, and consistent. For the purposes of a proposal, it should document painstaking library and Internet research and have a fair balance between academic books and journals.

 FINAL CHECKLIST

○ Divide the proposal into sections and list the tasks in each section that you will have to carry out to finish the document.

○ Try to shape the first few paragraphs so that sentences move from general to specific.

○ Begin with an overview and background and then set forth the problem, citing sources that agree that it is an issue.

○ Describe a debate in terms of opposing sides. Alternatively, pinpoint a gap in the literature, a faulty assumption, or evidence that has been overlooked or misinterpreted.

○ Draft and redraft your research question so it is clear, direct, and answerable within the parameters of the study.

○ Formulate a hypothesis that anticipates the results or frames the thesis so it can be tested.

○ Create a preliminary thesis statement that outlines the arguments or the expected conclusion. Continue to craft the thesis statement as the research continues.

○ Explain why your study is important in the statement of significance.

○ Develop two or three main objectives for the research.

○ If your study revolves around several key terms, consult the best authorities and then reference them to create your own definition.

○ State your assumptions explicitly.

○ Develop the outline to the argument.

○ Identify two or three bodies of literature that you will bring together to answer your research question.

○ Write the literature review with an introduction, a mini-essay summarizing and critiquing each of the bodies of literature you reference, a results section, and a conclusion. Build effective transitions between all of these parts to make the literature review a cohesive unit.

○ Develop your methodology by critically assessing the methods used by previous scholars. Explain the approach you will use to collect data and interpret it.

○ Identify available digital technologies and explain how you will integrate them into your methodology.

○ Concentrate on developing a comprehensive bibliography that is uniformly formatted according to one of the major style guides.

Chapter Summary

This chapter listed components of a proposal, the relationships among the parts, and how they come together to produce a document that gets your project approved by your professor or thesis committee. We offered a compressed summary of the different pieces and how they are ordered to produce a coherent research project. We explained as well that the proposal shows your professors the research you have carried out so far and what you plan to do to complete the project. The proposal also serves as your own blueprint so you know what work you must carry out to finish your project.

7

Research and New Technologies

Chapter Outline ⦿

As technology changes the way we research, write, create, and disseminate knowledge, scholarly documents are becoming increasingly **multimodal**. Academic writing now incorporates still and moving images, music, sound effects, voices, and computational and interactive structures in ways that move beyond traditional text-based paradigms of scholarship. Chapter Seven explains some of the ways that new technologies are altering scholarly production. We describe the digital essay, discuss the level of formality expected in academic writing, and distinguish modelling from plagiarism. We describe more fully how to go about designing a project that meets the standards for excellence in a discipline. We also discuss the role of theories and methods, explain the concept of abstracting, and suggest that early on, you begin thinking about the theoretical and methodological frameworks for your study.

Research and New Technologies

Re-searching—the process of mastering a subject by searching for and examining all of its facets again and again from many different points of view and then documenting your findings—is, in one sense, the process scholars have been employing for millennia to examine a subject in ways that lead to understanding and insight. Today, however, advances in technology have provided electronic tools that radically reduce the time it takes to conduct research. These advances also suggest new modalities for documenting your intellectual work.

This is an exciting time to be a researcher! We are in the midst of a great rethinking about the dynamic relationship of form to content in scholarship. This rethinking centres on the ways that technology is re-configuring infrastructures, social and cultural interactions, and scholarly routines in academic research. Old rules of scholarship are being challenged, and new approaches are in the process of formation. As the momentum of the shift from print to new media accelerates, it will become progressively more common for professors to ask you to employ digital technologies to create interactive scholarly texts.

Digital Writing

Digital writing is more than print practices carried over to computer environments. You will have to understand how to integrate pictures, video, audio, and animation with alphabetic writing to create a unified format. As you do, you will be creating your own digital project and you will also be helping to define the parameters, lay the foundations, and build the frameworks for the kinds of techniques and procedures that will be part of the everyday toolkits of tomorrow's researchers.

Old and New Academic Genres

The various academic disciplines employ distinct theories, methods, and approaches to documenting knowledge that have developed over a long-term history of institutional usages, practices, and conventions. These traditions of scholarship have led to discipline-specific **genres** of literature and media. Genres are customs, rules, and styles that situate modes of inquiry within a specific discipline and tradition of writing.

These different styles and forms for communicating information have evolved over time to represent knowledge efficiently and effectively to readers and audiences in a specific field. When scholars in a discipline study visual or textual documents, the common background they share leads them to expect that they will encounter certain discipline-specific codes, approaches, and strategies such as: the physics essay, history paper, marketing report, fine arts review, or the case study.

Genres and Interdisciplinary Research

At the same time, the trend to interdisciplinary research has started to erode boundaries that have compartmentalized knowledge into separate domains in the academy. Disciplines and their respective genres are being combined in new ways in interdisciplinary research. ●⟩

Today, long-standing patterns of disciplinary scholarship persist alongside new conventions and interdisciplinary methods for communicating information. In integrating scholarship and digital media, your goal will be to create a new kind of academic genre that synthesizes established styles in your discipline even as it incorporates some conventions from other disciplines with new digital technologies.

The Hybrid Multimedia Essay

Start thinking now about ways your project might meld conventional scholarly research in your field with findings from other areas of scholarship. Add to this the use of databases that archive information, multimedia presentations, and links to digital manuals, reference works, guides, indexes, hypertext articles, or geographic information.

Today it is still somewhat rare for students to submit hybrid documents that blend the traditional discipline-specific essay with research from other academic domains as well as new media. In future, these sorts of documents promise to be much more common. So now is a great time to learn how to construct a digital essay. ●⟩

The Digital Essay

The digital essay is a new kind of document created by using the tools, methods, and media made possible by new developments in communication and information technologies. The word *essay* is derived from the French *essayer*, which means to try or to attempt. It stems from the Latin *exigere*—to drive out, to try, or to examine. In the English language, the term *essay* first meant a trial or an attempt. The format for student essays emerged over several centuries and continues to evolve.

As a formal expression representing learning and acquired knowledge, student essays set forth and emphasize information in ways that disciplinary bodies approve and expect. If an essay satisfies traditional standards and criteria and then goes beyond them by offering digital enhancements that enrich the scholarship, it will stand out from the competition. A carefully constructed and thoughtfully argued hyperlinked essay that includes images, sounds, and video footage is in a separate category from the black and white printed pages submitted by other students in the class. Producing a unique product that exceeds expectations positions your study for top marks!

So again, your first priority is to make sure your digital essay satisfies the criteria for scholarly writing in your primary discipline even as it draws on material from other research areas and employs new digital techniques and tools. ◐

Discipline-Specific Genres

To understand what we mean by discipline-specific genres, it is instructive to consider how the sciences developed and became established as disciplinary departments in the academy. From the beginning of the modern era up to the early twentieth century, the sciences were still in the process of evolving into disciplines. As new and emerging subject areas, the sciences were not immediately accepted into the framework of traditional academic disciplines and were considered renegade fields of inquiry. During this time the sciences were not subcategorized into distinct disciplines such as astronomy, chemistry, and physics. In fact, scientific research was excluded from standard university curricula in both Europe and North America.

In response to this exclusion, those working in areas we now regard as the sciences developed learned societies that met regularly to facilitate the exchange of ideas. These associations began to publish academic journals to disseminate research findings. Over time, the style of writing in scientific disciplines developed systematic conventions aimed at objective standards and reproducible methods. As the sciences were accepted as distinct disciplines and rose in prominence in the academy, writing styles became formalized and eventually institutionalized in generic forms. Today, the sciences are considered premier disciplines in the university, and the discipline-specific conventions developed for scholarly writing in physics, astronomy, chemistry, and other subject areas have influenced academic writing in nearly every other discipline (Gibson 2009).

Voice and Objectivity

In what ways have the sciences had an impact on other disciplinary genres? Objectivity has been emphasized as a crucial feature of the scientific method. As a result, literary conventions that minimize the personality and quirks of the individual researcher became institutionalized as generic forms of documentation—genres—in scientific research. One example would be the use of the passive voice (e.g., "Mistakes were made" as opposed to "I made a mistake"). Constructions such as "The researchers decided to adapt available methods" rather than "We adapted available methods" downplayed the subjective dimension in observations and therefore became a standard convention in essay writing in the so-called hard sciences (e.g., physics, astronomy, and chemistry).

Subjective Voice

Passionate arguments, viewpoints influenced by personal circumstances, and perspectives gained from experience were all perceived as lacking objectivity. When this stylistic convention of the objective voice was taken up by other disciplines, students were discouraged from developing a personal writing style. More recently, changes in stylistic standards have opened the door to a voice that employs the first-person singular—that is, the use of words such as *I* or *my*.

Mixed Voice

There is also a trend to the use of hybrid forms that combine both objective and subjective voices (e.g., "This study shows . . . so I argue . . . " or "The experiment demonstrates . . . I therefore concur with previous studies that have . . ."). In writing your research essay and digital project, you will need to be aware of these conventions in order to ensure your work connects with your professor and other readers in the field who are your target audience. Recognizing and mastering the generic forms and conventions in a discipline is a significant step toward achieving academic success and, perhaps, eventual publication of your research results.

What Do All Essays Have in Common?

Though every discipline has specific requirements for scholarly writing, there are some overarching features that essays in all disciplines have in common. The style of writing most frequently used in all disciplines in higher education is the argumentative form. In your research, you will be gathering the material you will need to create and support a persuasive case. In other words, you will be attempting or trying in your essay to bring together all the facts and evidence you can muster in order to construct a compelling argument that will convince readers to accept your findings, change their minds, or adopt your point of view.

RESEARCH IN ACTION · Jamila's story

Jamila knew she wanted to be an investigative journalist and that she was interested in various conventions of journalistic writing, even as she was challenged in her English literature course by an assignment that included a digital component. As she conducted her research, she acquired more information and began to form a design for the kind of paper she would write.

After researching the work of various practitioners, Jamila learned that journalists write in a number of different styles. She noticed that one genre, which was based on principles of literary theory, had more of a narrative style than others and that the writer was often inserted into the story. So in addition to researching areas of investigative journalism, Jamila began looking at self-reflective narrative theory and kept her eyes open for a particular case study to use as a model for a digital project.

Jamila was intrigued by a recent movie she had seen that discussed gonzo, a genre of reporting invented by Hunter S. Thompson, a *Rolling Stone* magazine reporter. At a time when reporters did not identify themselves within the news story because it was thought to detract from unbiased reporting, Thompson pioneered the style of journalism that incorporates the active voice or first-person narrative. He placed himself, as narrator, at the centre of the story.

Thinking about Hunter S. Thompson led Jamila to create a first-person narrative documentary script of the best articles on gonzo journalism that she found online. Her final digital project involved comparative studies of the blogs and vlogs of twelve eminent investigative journalists. She noted the similarities and differences in their narrative styles and then mashed up a short video highlighting the techniques that various professionals used to introduce themselves as subjects in their own articles.

Formality and Argument

One convention of academic writing that is fairly constant across disciplines is a certain formality in the language of presentation. As a rule, scholarly papers do not rely on contractions. Your study should state that "it cannot be the case . . ." rather than "it can't be the case . . ." or "it does not follow . . ." instead of "it doesn't follow . . . ." As you review the documents you uncover in your research, pay attention to these and other subtleties in the language used by authors to express their arguments and to communicate how they understand, interpret, and weigh evidence; then deploy these linguistic formalities to build a convincing case.

In terms of constructing an argument, continually ask yourself how the essays and articles you are reading present facts, evaluate evidence, analyze the strengths or weaknesses of competing arguments, identify gaps in knowledge, and establish context. Pay particular attention to the techniques used by leading authorities to build a case and construct an argument that is more persuasive, defensible, and indeed superior to the arguments of other researchers who examine the same problems and issues.

Collecting Model Studies

As you progress with the research and begin to identify the best scholarly works, both in your discipline and in other fields, consider building a collection of these stellar examples that you can use as **models**—works that supply a plan, paradigm, pattern, or blueprint for mapping, organizing, and constructing your own original study. As you review the studies produced by different scholars, you will see recurring patterns in the way that information is organized and represented. How do the studies referenced by many leading authorities introduce their topics? At what point in the essay do they present the research question? How do they contextualize the problem/s they describe? In a standard journal article, what is the length of a particular component relative to the whole essay? How do top scholars deal with data collection and interpretation? How do they organize a conclusion?

Abstracting Common Features from Many Essays

From the many specific essays that you read, try to **abstract** features common to all excellent essays as well as the distinct conventions that are specific to your main disciplines. *Abstract* descends from the Latin word meaning to draw away, extract, or remove, and denotes a withdrawing or separating from physical or material embodiment, practices, or specific examples.

By abstracting a general form from many books and papers written by a number of prominent scholars, you will be able to discern the features that characterize scholarly writing more generally or in interdisciplinary research as well as those that serve as the formal standard for essays in one discipline—and imitate them in your own writing.

Components of the Essay

Attend to the way an academic essay is a compound document made up of multiple components (e.g., the title, introduction, footnotes, methodology, and bibliography). Likewise, a quality research study typically provides background or a context that gives an overview and includes a Review of Literature and a Methodology section. It details the way the investigation was conducted, highlights results and implications, and brings the study to a close by giving an account of the insights gained from the research.

Reading widely will help you begin to absorb intuitively the basic elements that all academic essays share even as you concentrate on making some of these features explicit. In addition, breaking your digital essay assignment down into components will make your project more manageable and reduce your sense of being overwhelmed as a deadline approaches.

Integrating New Media

Beyond the scholarly traditions of research and writing that determine the overall form of your essay and the logic of how you structure your arguments, you need to think about the media you will employ. How can you use hypertext, links, images, and sound to interest and impress your reader? Make a list of the technical skills you will need to acquire in order to achieve the aims of the project you are envisioning. Check with the university to see if specialized software programs (e.g., PhotoShop or Adobe Creative Suite) are available to students at a discounted rate. ◉

As your vision of the project takes shape, you will find yourself adjusting the components of your project. Even in the final stages, when all the elements are in place and you are polishing your project, you will likely need to continue doing some research in order to tweak and improve your product.

Clarify Expectations for the Assignment Descriptions with the Professor ◉

Having a thorough understanding of the professor's expectations for the assignment is an important early step. Try to gather as much information as you can about the criteria for assessing the essay. Ask for additional instructions. Communicate with the professor and ask questions about the purpose of the assignment and the criteria that will be used to assess the work. Talk to other students in the class to see what they think is required.

Understanding an Assignment

Did the professor distribute written instructions for the assignment? Have you read them many times to gain a thorough grasp of the purpose of the assignment and therefore what is required? If you have read the instructions over and over and are still not clear about what your teacher wants, do not immediately assume the problem lies with you. Some professors are brilliant writers and others are not great. As a beginning scholar, it will be difficult for you to distinguish one from the other. In either case, if you do not have an exact understanding of what the person who will be grading your work expects, you will have a difficult time producing a piece of work that meets those expectations and therefore earns a top grade.

Online Audiences

Beyond the expectations of your professor, think about how to make your work appeal to a wider community of readers. Identify the digital tools and techniques you will bring to bear on your project. Think about what might impress your readers and convince them of your mastery over the material. What are the basics that absolutely need to be covered? How can you make your study stand out from the work of other capable students? Does the discipline in general place a higher priority on originality or on competent execution?

Overly Ambitious Projects

Many students take on projects that are too ambitious both for the size specified by professors and the time available. Stay within the guidelines your professor gave you regarding the number of words you are to write. Remember, it is better to produce a superb analysis of a small aspect of a problem than to tackle a major issue and then find you only have time to deal with it in a limited fashion.

A Tried-and-True Strategy

You will seldom go wrong if you (1) identify the questions and problems that are the focus of current discussion and debate among the most respected authorities at the leading edge of a field; (2) break these questions and problems down into components; and (3) concentrate on shedding some light on one small component. By tackling one small element of a much larger issue, your goal is to provide a fresh take on your question through detailed analysis, critique, and your own original insights.

Modelling

We have suggested that you collect excellent essays that can serve as models for your own projects. Modelling involves looking to the best work as exemplars and prototypes for your own theories, methods, writing, arguments, and digital projects. Modelling adopts, adapts, and transforms the contents created by another writer into a new synthesis that is uniquely your own. It subjects the material to a total metamorphosis. The form remains even as the content is converted into something radically distinctive by substituting the material you are investigating for the material discussed by the author you are modelling.

When you model your project after exemplary studies, you abstract the salient features while studiously avoiding copying the particular content of any one work. When you do keep someone else's words and ideas without putting them through a process of translation, you reference this material appropriately through the use of quotation marks, footnotes, endnotes, or parenthetical citations.

Plagiarizing versus Modelling

In contrast to modelling, plagiarizing involves borrowing or copying contents wholesale without properly attributing ideas to their source with quotation marks and footnotes or endnotes. Plagiarizing involves reproducing word-for-word phrases, sentences, images, or ideas and inserting them into your own document. To be specific, plagiarizing entails *stealing* the words, sounds, or notions of others without any translation of the contents or acknowledgement that they are not of your own invention.

Summarizing someone else's ideas without citing the source is plagiarism. Paraphrasing someone else's content without referencing the original text is plagiarism. Whereas modelling involves a complete change of words, ideas, rhythms, styles, and patterns so that the material becomes your own even as it fits into the established forms and conventions for scholarly writing, plagiarizing involves taking ideas without crediting the person or persons who created them.

When you model your research after an excellent visual or written text, you are mixing, morphing, and sculpting information so that it fits into the generic forms for your discipline. When you plagiarize, you take someone else's material and attempt to deceive the reader into thinking it is your own original work.

Mashups and Remixes

Digital projects often mash up or remix previous materials to create a new piece of work. While contents are often taken up without attribution on the Internet, in a scholarly study you need to be doubly aware of how critical it is to cite the sources of your material and acknowledge when ideas are not your own. Even in cases of **satire**, when a person or a text is imitated in order to poke fun or to ridicule, you must be scrupulous about citing your sources or risk being accused of cheating.

Disciplines as Discourse Communities

Disciplines create **discourse communities**—scholarly groups that draw on particular theories, methods, ideas, information, texts, and techniques as background to the study of certain phenomena (e.g., Precambrian fossils, DNA, or insects). Discourse communities share certain approaches to their subject matter. When a number of scholars examine a subject over time, they extrapolate patterns of similarity from a variety of specific cases to create broad theories that explain why things work the way they do in a specialized area. The study of many instances of a phenomenon leads to the establishment of methods and techniques that then come to form the basis of disciplinary specialization.

Theories and Methods

From the first moment you begin thinking about a project, you need to consider the theories and methods you will employ. While there are some general theories and methods, many are specific to a discipline. As scholars in a field concentrate on observing similar phenomena over time, they focus on certain areas and ignore others. They concentrate on gaining a comprehensive understanding of a certain area in order to develop general theories that explain what specific observations have in common.

For example, sociologists use various methods to examine the behaviour of particular groups of people or populations in order to generate theories about how individuals come together and interact. Political scientists use various tools and techniques that allow them to focus on the power dynamics among specific individuals and groups in a society in order to develop overall theories about leadership.

Theories

A **theory** is a set of interconnected notions, ideas, rules, or principles that together describe, explain, or provide an account of some thing, situation, or phenomenon based on general laws or rules that exist independently of the thing under scrutiny. A theory sometimes suggests or even justifies a course of action based on what is possible or should happen.

Theory is descended from the Greek word *theoria*, which references a mental process of observing, viewing, contemplating, or looking at many specific examples and then drawing away or abstracting more general principles that apply to all alike. For example, observing the kinds of nests, dens, and architectural structures constructed by both animals and humans in a particular geography over time might lead to the theory that "the forms of shelter created by living beings in this region are in part a response to a climate with high temperatures and a high level of rainfall."

In an academic essay, a **theoretical framework** is the component of the document that sets forth and makes explicit the system of principles that serve as the constructs that will be used to provide an account of the phenomena under investigation. A strong theoretical frame will supply the general rules that allow you to interpret information, weigh and evaluate arguments, and justify the approach you are taking when you offer your own response to the concerns you are identifying in your research.

Methods and Methodologies ◉))

A **method** is a procedure, instrument, technique, tool, or manner of data collection used to study facts or evidence. A **methodology** involves something more than simply a method. A methodology entails describing, explaining, assessing, or critiquing the standard processes, concepts, theories, or methods associated with your discipline. Moreover, a methodology involves examining or questioning the reasons or assumptions that form the intellectual underpinning of a specific theory or method. As an example, "scientific method" is the name of the method in the study of evidence in disciplines such as physics, biology, chemistry, and pharmacology. The methodology might examine systematically the fundamental assumptions, premises, intellectual underpinnings, logic, and coherence of the scientific method itself as an approach.

As a rule, every academic study should include a few sentences to several paragraphs explaining the methodology as one significant component of the overall project.

FINAL CHECKLIST

- ○ Formulate a solid understanding of what the professor expects you to accomplish with the assignment.
- ○ Outline ways to meet the expectations of your professor at the same time as you try to make your work appeal to a wider audience on the Internet.
- ○ With an outline of the requirements and expectations for the assignment, identify the steps you will need to take in order to satisfy all of the criteria.
- ○ Determine the basics that need to be covered and work on these areas as a first priority.
- ○ Identify the genre or interdisciplinary genres that characterize good writing in your discipline and select key studies to serve as models.
- ○ Begin to examine a number of examples of the digital tools and techniques you will use for your project; itemize the steps you need to take to learn new skills to bring your envisioned digital essay to completion.
- ○ Make sure you have observed the appropriate formalities in your study.
- ○ Gather evidence and weigh arguments in the literature in order to put together a strong, persuasive case for your own study.
- ○ Identify ideas or concepts in the literature that you can analyze and critique in order to contribute your own theories, methods, arguments, and ideas.
- ○ Plan to divide the project into smaller components and work on refining and improving each of the parts; then integrate everything so that you submit a polished final project.
- ○ Make sure you credit all your sources of inspiration by citing appropriately.
- ○ Regularly repeat all the steps in your research so that you gradually work toward completing a stellar project.

Chapter Summary

The digital essay is a multimodal document that integrates scholarship with new technological tools and media forms. Digital creativity is more than print practices moved to electronic documents; digital essays are interactive texts that synthesize words, images, audio files, databases, and other components into a unified format.

Every discipline relies on theories, methods, and models that create distinctive genres for scholarly communication. Each genre acts as a marker of agreement and consensus among scholars working in a particular discipline. Interdisciplinary genres bring together in one study the standards, practices, procedures, and findings of more than one discipline. Accordingly, the digital essay is a hybrid or mixed form that merges a traditional genre with new formats made possible by innovations in communication and information technology, and so it must meet the standards expected in more than one discipline.

An essay is a kind of formal trial. To succeed, you must demonstrate mastery over a subject area while at the same time exploiting the potential of digital media to enhance your presentation. Consider the conventions and styles prevalent in your discipline, and adjust the form of your project to meet the expectations of your discourse community.

Study excellent examples of writing and creative work, both in your discipline and in other subject areas. Find exemplars that can serve as models to guide the way you might organize your material.

A theory is a consistent and coherent system of thought involving interlinked ideas or principles that describe or explain some phenomena by way of general laws or rules. The theoretical framework of your project will provide the overall parameters within which you can interpret and assess the particular case you are investigating.

A method is a specific tool, technique, or procedure for gathering data and analyzing evidence. By contrast, the methodology explains, tests, or questions the basic assumptions that underlie theories or methods.

8

Planning and Drafting

Chapter Outline

Chapter Eight describes and explains the major features that characterize the kinds of writing typical of scholarly essays. We give directions for writing abstracts that stand at the beginning of many academic articles and book chapters and serve as proposals for acceptance at scholarly meetings and conferences. We also explain the difference between a thesis and a capstone project. Strategies for integrating your scholarship and digital media help you to develop a compelling project. We list associations and professional journals that can serve as resources for identifying the features characterized by excellent writing across the disciplines. We also list guides to the conventions that signal excellence in your particular field. As you delve more deeply into the research, we offer advice on evaluating the quality of the material you discover.

Major Kinds of Scholarly Essays

There are many different kinds of scholarly essays. Here we briefly touch on the most significant formats.

Hamburger Essay

The five-paragraph "hamburger essay" is often taught as a model for academic essay writing. In the hamburger model, the Introduction is compared to the top of the bun; the second through fourth paragraphs are the "meat and trimmings" because each one discusses a major point; and then the fifth paragraph, like the bottom of the bun, rounds out the essay and holds it together with the Conclusion. This standard five-paragraph format is most frequently taught in high school. When you begin university studies, you are expected to be able to structure your writing in this manner.

However, we do not recommend the hamburger model for essays in higher education. In fact, we cannot emphasize enough that the five-paragraph essay is a rigid format that leaves little room for exploring and investigating the actual parameters of a subject. Instead, we recommend that you allow the overall approach and structure of your study to emerge from the research.

The Argumentative Essay

The argumentative piece aims to persuade the reader to adopt the position put forward by the author. The **persuasive argument** is a common format for scholarly writing across all the disciplines. Academic essays typically seek to shape communication in ways that help bring about a voluntary change in readers' minds, turning their thinking around so they accept a position they did not hold before.

Persuading Readers

There are three major ways to change the minds of readers. The first is to gain their trust. The second is to appeal to their emotions. And the third is to supply valid reasons that convince them to adopt your point of view based on the logic of the argument.

There are a number of common types of persuasive arguments; techniques for creating major premises; and ways to make inferences, to anticipate and refute the most common fallacies, and to address other problematic attempts at argumentation. ◉

Cause and Effect Essays

Cause and effect essays seek to identify the reasons why a certain action or event took place and to trace the effects that followed from it. Cause and effect essays are often used in legal scholarship and medical diagnoses.

Classification or Definition Essays

The classification or definition piece aims to categorize and/or define an act, event, object, or subject. Traditional encyclopedia articles and Wikipedia entries are examples of this format.

The Comparison and Contrast Essay

The comparison and contrast essay is a format that is used in a number of disciplines. Comparison works by analogical reasoning. Essays of this kind conduct a parallel examination of two things, typically one being more well known so that it serves as a basis for comparison with the lesser-known thing. In your study you set two or more texts, acts, events, or objects side by side. Briefly describe the differences in context, time frame, or other factors that are unique to each comparator. Next, identify common features, and then investigate the similarities and differences between the common attributes.

The Critical Essay

The word *critical* is descended from a Greek word meaning to choose, separate, or discern. The **critical** essay is a piece of writing that seeks to investigate, analyze, interpret, and evaluate a topic. Its purpose is not to find fault with a topic so much as to assess and evaluate it from a position of non-biased, detached reflection. The critical essay is one of the most common formats for interpreting works of literature, film, or other media. In the case of a film review, for example, major components of the critical essay might include an examination of the movie's elements— situation, characters, conflict, themes, plot, structure, symbols, irony, point of view, or voice—and an assessment of whether these facets of the production come together in a unified whole.

Deductive Reasoning Essay

The essay based on **deductive reasoning** states one or more facts, principles, or assumptions (premises) and then makes observations in light of them to reach a conclusion. In deductive arguments, the premise/s are linked to the conclusion. If all of the premises are true and the words are clear and precise, then the conclusion is necessarily true. Here is a famous example:

> Premise one: All humans are mortal.
> Premise two: Socrates is a human.
> Conclusion: Socrates is mortal.

The conclusion is reached after you have examined the premises. The first premise states that all those things categorized as human are mortal (they are born and eventually die). The second premise observes that Socrates is a member of the human species. The conclusion is then that Socrates must necessarily be mortal because he shares the attribute of mortality with all humans. In deductive essays, the conclusion follows from the premises.

Inductive Reasoning Essay

In the essay based on **inductive reasoning**, the premises add weight to the probability or likelihood that the conclusion is true. There can be several premises, each of which contributes to the overall likelihood of the conclusion, even though the conclusion does not necessarily follow from the premises.

In contrast to a deductive argument, where the truth or falsity of conclusions is tied to the premises, the conclusion in an inductive argument may not follow from the premises. Whereas in deductive arguments the conclusion is reached from general statements or premises, the conclusion is an inductive argument is reached from particular examples. In deductive arguments, the conclusion is either valid or invalid. In inductive arguments, conclusions can be weaker or stronger. Here is a simple example of an inductive argument:

> My friend Jim just won the lottery.
> Premise one: Jim told me he plans to share his winnings with friends and family.
> Premise two: Jim offered to pay for our lunch today.
> Premise three: Jim left our indifferent server a large tip.
> Conclusion: Jim is probably a generous person.

You can see that the three premises are separate from one another and that each one provides additional support or weight to the conclusion, though they do not logically follow from one another and show the conclusion to be true. It is still possible that the conclusion is false. Jim is likely a generous person but he is not necessarily generous in all circumstances. If you are writing an inductive essay, you concentrate on providing evidence that supports a conclusion and on providing counter examples to refute the evidence that weighs against a conclusion.

Exploratory Essay

When you write an exploratory essay, you begin without having an end or conclusion in mind. The exploratory piece takes as a starting point your lack of knowledge and the absence of a formulated opinion on a topic. This format commits you to following the direction the research suggests without having any preconceived notion of what the outcome will be. Thus, the exploratory essay involves researching and writing to learn something rather than to make a point or argue a case.

Expository Essay

Expository writing presents a full and accurate account of the views of others or reports on the facts concerning issues or events. **Exposition** clarifies and illuminates a topic by providing a thorough description that avoids bias, opinion, critique, or argument.

Narrative Essay

A narrative essay tells a story through the lens of the author's personal experiences.

Purposes of Research Essays

All the preceding essay formats incorporate research. Much of what is expected of you throughout your years as a university student will involve organizing your thinking effectively in various formats such as term projects, theses, and capstone projects. Research essays have two related purposes. First, they provide you with an opportunity for independent study and with the experience of identifying, organizing, and developing information on a topic. Second, they are practical exercises in mastering the conventions of academic writing and bibliographic documentation. The twofold functions of research papers are what make them a basic requirement for college or university work almost everywhere.

Abstract

Many academic studies include an **abstract**—typically a six- to ten-sentence outline that "draws away" or summarizes the key aspects of your entire paper. Abstracts are placed at the beginning of your essay to outline the parameters of your study.

Abstracts as Proposal Documents

Abstracts are frequently requested as proposals for conference presentations or contributions to collections, anthologies, or special issues that focus on a theme or a problem. In these instances, abstracts are a form of promise for a presentation or an essay that you have not yet written. For this reason, abstracts require careful formulation so that you can deliver the full-length study you said you would submit.

When written before the essay has been completed, superior abstracts outline the problem, theoretical framework, and methodology, and they give a sense of the analysis, indicate the results, and set forth the thesis. When written after the essay has been completed, the abstract also presents the conclusion to your study.

The abstract is often a "ticket for admission" to scholarly events or publications, in that it provides a thumbnail sketch of the entire project you are proposing; the better you can make this paragraph, the more likely it is that you will be invited to participate in the scholarly event or activity.

Try beginning with an intriguing statement of the problem so you capture the interest of your readers and they understand how you are positioning your research on a topic. Try to indicate the theoretical framework and methods you will use. The more information about the study that you can condense into the abstract, the more likely it is that you will be asked to create the full-length study.

Abstracts as Summaries

Not only is the abstract a key vehicle for acceptance to events and publications, it is also the major source of information about your completed piece once it has been published. Many anthologies of essays and peer-reviewed journals place an abstract at the beginning of the essay so readers know what the writing is about. Having a clearly written abstract ensures that you will encourage as many scholars as possible to obtain your essay and, ultimately, cite it in their own research.

Making a Major Project More Manageable

Significant research essays have multiple components. An abstract is one of many separate elements that need to come together to create a major project—the others being the Introduction, Review of Literature, Methodology, Analysis or Body, Results or Findings, Conclusion, Bibliography, and Appendix. Each part must be completed, polished, and integrated into the whole to create a successful piece of work.

As a complex project, the essay can be divided into sections to make completing the entire study more manageable. Are you feeling overwhelmed or having trouble getting started? Concentrate on smaller, easier-to-deal-with units, and finish each one to a high standard. Then, shift your focus to the big picture and bring all the pieces together to construct a unified finished project. ◉〉

Term Project

It is worthwhile having a clear idea about the differences between various kinds of projects. Term projects are typically scholarly research essays that require a significant commitment of time and energy throughout the semester—usually the entire term. Many university courses require an academic essay that involves a literature review, data collection and analysis, results, and conclusions—as well as some form of creative outcome. Employing digital media has a major influence over how term projects are organized.

Nonlinear Digital Projects

Designing an essay that incorporates hypertext, links, images, sound, and other digital features will force you to think about how your readers might approach your text in nonlinear ways. What happens if they open your document in the middle, flip or click to the Bibliography, then move on to the Table of Contents? Have you made sure to bring all the parts of your study up to the same standard so that readers have a favourable impression no matter how they choose to read your study?

Thesis

There are two different senses of the word **thesis**. At the most basic level, a thesis is a statement that introduces and summarizes the content of an essay by presenting the main argument, claims, ideas, or conclusion. On a larger level, a thesis is a term for a study that is longer and more complex than a term paper but not as large and complex as a doctoral dissertation or a book.

Writing a thesis means you will likely be engaged for one or more semesters in intensive research on a piece of work that presents a sustained argument over many pages. In fact, writing a thesis is so challenging that it often substitutes for up to a year of university courses in a program.

What Makes an Excellent Thesis?

Good theses are delimited, coherent, and rigorous. To be delimited, the scope of the project must be restricted to providing relevant information. This is information that can be covered in the space available without moving away from the main arguments to deal with material that is related by only one or two threads.

To be coherent, all the parts of the study must come together in a unity that expresses one idea. Information that is not necessary should be removed, leaving only the statements that are crucial to the argument.

Finally, a thesis should be rigorous and precise. In other words, the argument should be focused so that it leads to one interpretation only.

A thesis requires an understanding of method. In this sense, it sets up a system for analysis, applies that system to a particular subject in order to see what happens, formulates results, and then arrives at conclusions. The methodology is what makes a thesis unique. If you want to ensure that new media are fully integrated into your thesis, the inclusion of digital media in the methodology for your project makes it easier to create such a synthesis.

Capstone Project

The capstone project is the major culminating creative assignment at the end of an undergraduate or master's degree that shows how you have absorbed and integrated all the material you have studied. Most often, the end of a university degree stipulates the capstone project and a research paper as evidence of theoretical research and applied practical skills. The capstone project is therefore typically related if not integrated with the thesis. The demands involved in producing capstone projects are high, so again, the capstone project serves as the equivalent of several courses toward the university degree.

RESEARCH IN ACTION · Jody's story

An assignment for the term paper in Jody's criminology course asked students to examine forms of capital punishment during a time period of their choosing. Jody's initial research uncovered an image from the past that represented the forms of punishment for sins in a European society controlled by the church. This engraving by Hieronymus Bosch (1450–1516) depicted tortured and condemned people.

Jody studied Bosch's depictions of punishment, and she employed them as a basis for further research on the instruments used in Western Europe during the early modern period. The research indicated that instruments of punishment were a reflection of both the level of technology during that time and the cultural fears, anxieties, and beliefs about punishment in the Christian church.

For her term project, Jody created a mashup using Bosch's artwork as well as other images of instruments of punishment. She then juxtaposed these with images of equipment for administering fatal injections. Her comparative essay provided visual and documentary evidence in support of the argument that emerged from her research, namely, that instruments of punishment and execution in both early modern and contemporary societies are a reflection of technological developments and of beliefs, nightmares, and the urge for revenge.

Associations, Journals, and eResources

To commence studying the questions and approaches deemed important by scholars so that you can begin creating a solid draft of your essay, study, thesis, or capstone project, we recommend you start by seeking information from academic associations, leading journals, and eResources. Today, library catalogues are available online, so you should be able to rely on the Internet to uncover much of this information.

Finding Professional Academic Associations

A professional academic association functions as "the voice of the discipline." Discipline-specific academic associations provide more valuable resources in comparison with professional, hobby, or special interest groups. Academic associations extend knowledge by facilitating the exchange of ideas among scholars.

Associations typically hold annual or biannual conferences and meetings where colleagues gather to present papers, get feedback on their work prior to publication, discuss their research with like-minded others, and visit the booths of major presses that publish scholarly studies in their area.

Academic associations work to achieve the following:

- strengthen the study and teaching of their disciplines;
- address the common concerns of their scholarly communities at local, national, and international levels;
- represent the profession in policy matters;
- provide timely and systematic coverage of research developments in the discipline;
- harness the labour required to circulate new scholarship and information;
- offer additional education and networking opportunities for scholars;
- organize professional development opportunities;
- provide access to valuable resources; and
- keep their membership informed on up-to-the-minute news— not to mention gossip!

In addition to their signature journals, associations frequently produce other publications, such as annual directories, bibliographies, and online resources (including links to conferences or related associations), as well as individual booklets that address professional concerns.

Academic associations are also excellent sources of information about state-of-the-art tools and methods for digital scholarship. Membership in disciplinary organizations typically offers direct access to special software and publications.

The Scholarly Societies Project

An excellent source for information about academic associations is the Scholarly Societies Project (www.lib.uwaterloo.ca/society), which facilitates access to information about scholarly societies around the world with data beginning in 1994. ◉

The website provides links to 4,157 scholarly societies and 3,832 websites, and it allows you to search by subject, country, language, and founding dates. For example, if you would like to search by subject, and you select *history*, you will find that there are 155 professional associations around the world that focus on historical fields. For communication and media studies, there are 37 results. Many of these organizations have links to external resources, which in turn will help you find other related organizations.

Examples of Associations in History and Media Studies

As examples, we highlight resources for disciplinary work in history and in communication and media studies.

History

For historians of all stripes, membership in the American Historical Association (AHA) provides online access to electronic versions of a number of materials, including *Perspectives on History*, a printed newsmagazine, as well as their official publication, *The American Historical Review* (AHR), a journal that brings together scholarship from every major field of historical inquiry. The AHR is published in February, April, June, October, and December.

As digital technologies revolutionize the creation of documents, they are also transforming the way scholarly associations carry out their business. Historians have been early adopters of new technologies. The AHA website (www.historians.org/pubs/ahr.cfm) provides valuable resources for producing digital projects. ◉

Communication and Media Studies

The Canadian Communication Association and the International Communication Association are leading professional bodies for scholars in communication and media studies. As a subset of this discipline, the Society for Cinema and Media Studies (SCMS), which can be found online at www.cmstudies.org, is a valuable organization for scholars interested in cinema. The SCMS describes itself as an organization for "students, researchers, instructors, and practitioners working in film, television, radio, digital technologies, and other media."

This organization publishes *Cinema Journal* as their official peer-reviewed periodical. The SCMS, along with the Popular Culture Association and the American Mobile Telecommunications Association, are just a few examples of the many associations based on more specialized fields of interest in the study of communication and media.

Identifying Relevant Associations

You can begin your search for associations and journals by simply entering the name of the discipline—*economics*, for example—into a search engine. However, a general search such as this will typically turn up thousands of results for related but perhaps not-so-relevant professional groups. Many of these results will be specific to a particular university, or they will yield disciplinary organizations aimed primarily at fostering collaboration among students rather than professional researchers. As in all online searches, the more specific you make your query, the more relevant the results.

A Clue to Appropriate Associations for Research in a Course

If your professor has an online biography or a curriculum vitae, look up the associations to which he or she belongs and use the information you find on those sites as guides for genres, styles, and standards that you might adopt for your own essay. Are any associations listed in the references and resources your professor provides with the syllabus for the course?

Blogs, wikis, and discipline-specific e-mail lists are also useful resources that will help you find information about upcoming conferences, different professional associations, and even opportunities for research and collaboration.

Discipline-Specific eJournals, eBooks, and Databases

Electronic information resources that you can access on the Web, either on or off campus (with a university library card), include **eJournals**, **eBooks**, and online **databases**. eJournals are electronic issues of journals and articles, either web versions of print documents or so-called born-digital publications. eBooks are electronic versions of printed books; some use a **Creative Commons** licence that makes information available without charge to anyone with a computer. Online databases provide electronic abstracts and indexes that allow you to search for specific journal articles or materials of particular interest. Some online databases provide access to complete journal articles or full-text versions of essays; others offer only an abstract of the article.

Read the abstracts, which will give you an idea of the content and the major argument presented in a publication. When you find an article that looks interesting based on the abstract, you can choose to either find the print version in the library or pay a fee to have the article delivered to your inbox electronically.

Another reason for looking at associations and journals is to help you identify models for your own writing. Since scholarly writing always follows the codes and conventions of particular disciplines, the essays linked to association websites are a quick way to find information about an organization and the style of academic writing in a field.

Evaluating Research Studies

Scholars have developed a number of techniques to evaluate print information, and the same criteria can be used to assess information found on the Internet.

Authorship

Authorship is perhaps the single most important criterion in evaluating information online. Who wrote the text? Whose interests do they represent? How qualified is the author to provide information on a topic? When you look for texts with critical value, you want to know the basis of the writer's authority. Do you recognize the author's name? Is the author cited by another scholar you trust? Did you find or link to the author's document from another document you know to be reliable? Does the document provide biographical information or links to another page that includes the author's position, institutional affiliation, and address?

The Publishing Body

The publishing body also helps you evaluate a document. With print documents, peer-review generally means that the author's manuscript has been screened in order to verify that it meets the standards or aims of the publisher. Not all print documents have gone through peer-review or even vetting or fact-checking by an editor. Is the document you are reading published by a press that you recognize? Does it provide the name of an organization? Is this organization recognized in the field you are studying, and is it qualified to address the topic? Are there headers, footers, or distinctive indicators that show the document to be part of an official academic or scholarly website?

Remember that typically, digital documents have not been inspected as carefully as printed texts. Are you able to contact the site webmaster? If not, can you link to a page that lists identifying information? Are you able to verify the identity of the server that hosts the document? Internet programs such as DNS Lookup and Whois can often be of help.

Point of View or Bias

Point of view or bias may slant or subtly shape an author's assumptions or the views presented in the material you consult. Be on guard for highly interpretative uses of data. Corporate websites often present information in the best possible light or veil data that is really an advertisement. Political organizations may misrepresent the views of the opposition. Check to see if the document is located on the server of an organization that has a clear stake in an issue.

Referral to and Knowledge of the Literature

Referral to and knowledge of the literature provides the context in which authors situate their work. Appropriate referencing reveals what information providers know about their discipline and its practices. Proper references make it easier for you to evaluate the level of scholarship or knowledge of trends in the area. Does the document provide related sources with proper attribution? Is there a bibliography? Does the author demonstrate knowledge of theories, schools of thought, or techniques typically considered suitable for the treatment of the subject? If the author is using a new theory or technique as a basis for research, does he or she discuss the value of this new approach or mention limitations? If the treatment of the subject is controversial, are other sides of the debate acknowledged?

Accuracy or Verifiability of Details

The accuracy or verifiability of details is an important part of the evaluation process, especially when you are attempting to assess material that is presented in a non-traditional way or the work of an unfamiliar author presented by an organization that is foreign to you. Does the author of a research document explain how the data was gathered? Is there an account of the theories and method/s used to interpret it? If the methodology is outlined in the document, is it appropriate to the discipline and topic and does it allow the study to be duplicated for purposes of verification or falsification? Digital documents have added value if they rely on other sources that are listed in a bibliography. Does the background information that the document presents come from sources you can look up and verify?

Currency

Currency refers to the timeliness of information. In printed documents, the date of publication is the first indicator of currency. For some types of information, currency is not an issue: authorship or place in the historical record is more important. For most other types of data, however, currency is extremely important, as is the regularity with which the data is updated.

To ascertain currency, apply the following criteria: does the document include the date/s when the information was gathered (e.g., "Based on 1990 US Census data")? If there is a need to add or refresh data, does the document include information on the regularity of updates? Does the text include a date of copyright? If no date is given in an electronic document, can you consult the directory to look up the date of the latest modification?

Prioritizing of Information on the Search Engine

Prioritizing of information on the search engine is a significant factor in evaluating the sources of information you garner from a web search. AltaVista, InfoSeek, or directories such as Yahoo or Google employ search engines that determine the order in which query results are listed. Some Internet search engines sell top space to advertisers. In some instances, it may be worthwhile consulting a watchdog site such as Search Engine Watch.

Remember as well that Internet search engines are not like the databases found in libraries. Library databases include subject headings, abstracts, and other evaluative information created by information professionals to make searching more accurate. Library databases also index more permanent and reliable information. The Internet has no comparable organizational systems.

The above criteria help set general standards for scholarship across the disciplines. Learn to evaluate information that you find on the Internet. Conversely, these criteria will be applied by others when finding, evaluating, and assessing your work.

Filtering Documents Found on the Internet

Establishing and learning criteria for filtering what you find on the Internet is a prerequisite to becoming a critical scholar of information in all forms. Information literacy and competency involves "casting a cold eye" (as William Butler Yeats stated) on every document you retrieve. Look for other sources that can authenticate or corroborate what you find. Learn to be skeptical. Doubt what you read. Be critical!

Remember that whereas peer-reviewed books, chapters, and articles have been edited and fact-checked by scholars, publishers, editors, and librarians, other resources found online have typically not been examined to the same degree and so you must be extra careful about relying on this information.

If there are no standard filters for ensuring the quality, reliability, and accuracy of materials posted on a website, be aware that the further you move outside the online resources of the university library and disciplinary associations, the more cautious and skeptical you need to be. Your search results will be the product of an uncontrolled environment—meaning you will always have to question the quality of the information in the absence of editing or fact-checking.

Questioning the Material

- Has the author formulated a problem or issue?
- Could the problem have been approached more effectively from another perspective?
- Is the thesis clearly defined? Is its significance (scope, value, ramifications, relevance) established?
- What is the research orientation (e.g., interpretive, critical, scientific, interdisciplinary)?
- What is the theoretical framework (e.g., historical, psychological, philosophical, feminist)?
- What is the relationship between the theory and the author's perspective?
- Has the literature relevant to the problem or issue been effectively evaluated?
- How good are the various components of the study design (e.g., population, intervention, outcome)?
- In material written for a popular readership, does the author use appeals to emotion, one-sided examples, or rhetorically charged language and tone?

- Is there an objective basis to the reasoning, or is the author merely "proving" what he or she already believes?
- How does the author structure the argument?
- How accurate and valid are the measurements?
- Is the analysis of the data correct and relevant to the research question?
- Can you deconstruct the flow of the argument to see whether or where it breaks down logically (e.g., in establishing cause–effect relationships)?
- Is the validity of conclusions based upon the data and analysis?
- In what ways does this book or article contribute to our understanding of the problem under study, and in what ways is it useful for practice?
- What are the strengths and limitations?
- How does this book or article relate to the specific thesis or question you are developing?

Drafting the Essay

The process of academic writing is nonlinear. Experienced scholars expect to research, write notes about their research, do more research, and rewrite their document dozens of times before submitting the final product. This implies that first drafts are just that—preliminary and subject to change. When you first begin drafting your essay, we suggest you aim to get as many of your ideas down as possible. You will have opportunities to return to what you have written and to revise it based on your subsequent research. In this sense, writing and research go hand in hand. Scholars cannot do one without the other.

  FINAL CHECKLIST

○ Find appropriate professional associations and their related academic journals—they will be among your most important and reliable resources.

○ Identify and apply the specific styles and conventions used in your discipline/s by looking at work produced by members of a relevant professional association.

Continued . . .

○ Look for important concepts and ideas and how they are explained and used. For example, if the concept *ideology* is used, how is it defined and employed by the author?

○ Look for factual material, data, and statistics that are used to support arguments.

○ Take note of the arguments made by the author. Why does the author hold a particular view or, conversely, not believe something? What methods does he or she employ?

○ Look for contrasts and comparisons that authors frequently embed in their texts. Make a chart that highlights them.

○ Does the author use examples? Are they relevant? Do they support assertions? Or are the examples too selective, neglecting other cases that might not support assertions?

○ Look for threads and topics that come up repeatedly and ask yourself why they are significant.

○ Does the writer offer any new insights that point out relationships among phenomena that other authors have overlooked? Are these insights valuable? Where do they lead you?

○ Do not expect to agree with everything an author writes. If you disagree, make sure you have valid reasons that you back up with evidence.

○ What examples have authors omitted that might reinforce or refute their claims?

○ Consider adaptations you can make. For example, essays on the nature of heroes and heroines in Greek mythology can sometimes be profitably applied to characters in popular media. You may not be able to find an article on a particular situation comedy, but you will find material on situation comedies in general and on humour that you can apply to your example.

○ What about the author's tone and style? What is distinctive about the author's voice? How important is style in convincing you to believe something?

○ From what sources do many authors quote? These sources are likely key references in the field. How do frequently cited authors provide a standard for further research in the field? What do these sources tell you about the author's point of view, politics, and values?

Chapter Summary

This chapter distinguished the attributes and approaches characteristic of the most common forms of scholarly writing. We discussed the criteria involved in producing term essays, theses, and capstone projects, and we suggested ways you might go about synthesizing a more traditional academic essay with digital media. In addition, we gave instructions for identifying and accessing the most appropriate scholarly associations and peer-reviewed journals as key resources for intellectual ideas in your discipline. The work of scholars linked to a disciplinary association's website provides models for you to follow when you are writing in that discipline.

Since texts available online often have not been subjected to the same editorial standards and quality controls as print documents, we provided suggestions for assessing the documents you locate on the Internet.

9

The Introduction

Chapter Outline

Chapter Nine provides more detailed information about the major elements of the essay and digital project. We encourage you to envision your digital essay as a cohesive unity. At this stage of the research, you should work on the various components of the project, concentrating on creating connections and transitions among the parts. The Introduction is a revised and refined version of the document you created for the proposal. This chapter focuses on a more detailed description of the components and how they fit together. A checklist outlines the sequence of writing the Introduction to the study and the relationships between research and practice.

Titles and Subtitles

The title of your essay should excite the curiosity of the reader and provide a précis of the research or a thumbnail sketch of the whole. Titles take a great deal of skill to write. Start working on yours as soon as you narrow your project, and continue refining and polishing it all the way through the writing process.

Why? The title functions as the headline to your study, the announcement, the calling card, or the masthead. It encapsulates in a few words the scope of the entire essay. And it stands as a reflection of your thoroughness, care, and level of scholarship. If your professor or readers are not impressed with the title of your essay, they will not want to read further. The title is a short construction. Make sure it sends the right signal: "This is an outstanding piece of work!"

Remember that academic titles most often have two parts: a title and a subtitle separated by a colon. The title should be no more than five or six words; it should provide a hint about the argument you will be making and pique readers' interest.

The subtitle provides a more technical summary of the subject of the study. If you are concentrating on a specific case study or exemplary text or group of texts as the focus of the project, you may want to include that information in the subtitle.

Drew Gilpin Faust's major work *Mothers of Invention: Women of the Slaveholding South in the American Civil War* is masterfully titled and subtitled. There is idiomatic resonance in the title—three words, *mothers of invention*—while the ten-word subtitle narrows the project to elite women who headed households that kept slaves in the southern United States during the American Civil War.

Notice that there is a link between the two parts. *Mothers of Invention* suggests that a major focus is on the role of women as mothers—of their own children and, metaphorically, of their slaves—and on how inventive they had to be in order to manage their households while their property was under siege and their husbands, fathers, and sons were off at war. In fact, *Mothers of Invention* encapsulates one of the major themes of the entire work and brings to mind a number of images that would be appropriate to accompany the text for a digital presentation of this work. In addition, the subtitle situates the study in a gender, economic unit, social problem, geographical location, political conflict, and time period. Notice as well that the subtitle answers all the classic questions: who, what, when, where, why, and how.

Another example of an excellent title is Monique Tschofen's *"Agents of Aggressive Order": Letters, Hands, and the Grasping Power of Teeth in the Early Canadian Torture Narrative* (2008). Tschofen's study concentrates on a peculiar genre of literature that involved stories about aboriginal savagery and torture in early Canada. These stories were published by Jesuit priests and became wildly popular with European audiences of the time period. The four-word title references the Europeans (the agents) who came to North America and set about ordering the culture of the New World in accordance with that of the Old World through the use of violence and other aggressive means.

The fourteen-word subtitle of Tschofen's essay lets the reader know that the author is going to focus her attention on the metaphorical and thematic connections among writing, hands, and teeth in torture narratives. A fourteen-word subtitle is long; this is close to the maximum length for a scholarly subtitle. Try to keep your own subtitle within this limit.

Both paper and electronic documents frequently have a separate title page. For your digital essay, think about how media might be used to enhance the title page or screen: What font would augment the piece? Would a mashup of images that circulated with torture narratives increase interest in Tschofen's study? What about accompanying maps of the territory or images of the handwritten documents? Would it be helpful to have a blog with a curated selection of texts and images with an accompanying essay as commentary?

The long-standing convention of a separate title page for a research document invites creativity when it comes to integrating your scholarship with digital media. How can you translate this generic convention into an inspiring opening web page for your digital essay? In all cases, good titles and title pages are the product of extended contemplation and repeated drafts.

Abstract

Major essays and theses typically require a 250- to 500-word abstract that presents a condensed summary of what the entire project is about, including the problem, theoretical framework, methods, data analyzed, results, and conclusions. ◗))

Introduction

The Introduction is the most important section of your paper (with the Conclusion probably the second most important). Many professors believe they can tell what grade they will assign a paper after they have read the first two or three paragraphs. Why? If the wording is unclear; if there are spelling, grammatical, or typographical errors; or if the Introduction is not carefully organized, the level of writing and scholarship is unlikely to improve in later parts of the essay.

Similarly, readers will be disinclined to read the entire essay if the Introduction fails to capture their attention. So make this section of your project one of the most polished portions of the paper. This does not mean that the middle of the document can be wobbly or garbled and the reader will not notice. What it means is that you need to immediately impress the person who has taken time to look over your work because you will lose them if the opening fails to reflect a carefully researched and ordered piece of writing. The Introduction need not be poetry—but it does need to show evidence of writing and rewriting so the wording is clear and accurate, sentences and paragraphs are thoughtfully structured, and ideas are well-considered and accurately expressed.

Proportionate Length of the Introduction

As a very loose guide, for a 7,000 word electronic document or a 20 to 25 page print essay, the Introduction is generally a maximum of 500 to 1,000 words, or 2 to 4 pages. The Introduction to an undergraduate, master's, or doctoral thesis would be scaled upwards in proportion to the size of the document. Again, we emphasize that these are only approximate lengths; the number of words on a project will vary depending on the topic and the discipline.

Parts of the Introduction

Most excellent introductions include the following elements:

- a problem and its context;
- references (either footnotes or endnotes);
- a concise research question;
- a statement of significance;
- a hypothesis (in some cases);
- a thesis statement;
- aims, objectives, or purposes;
- scope and limitations;

- definitions (if appropriate);
- assumptions; and
- a sketch of the sections of the argument.

Ordering the Parts of the Introduction

There are many different ways these parts of the Introduction may be ordered and arranged. Some essays begin with a question, for example. Others start off with the problem and then provide more context a few paragraphs later. The statement of significance can appear before or after the thesis statement or even later in the Introduction. The point is that these elements are guidelines to the scholarly genre, and they can be put together in many ways depending on the topic and what seems to come naturally to you as you shape your argument.

Problem

Open the Introduction with one to three paragraphs that set forth the problem or issues you will address. These paragraphs typically establish the "big picture" and then move from general to specific. Start with a statement of the broad area related to the problem, then offer a few sentences that (1) go more deeply into the matter or (2) recount the background information and the main facts that are crucial to understanding the issues in context.

Citing Sources for Your Problem

Your paragraphs outlining the problem should reference several sources (whether in parenthetical citations, footnotes, or endnotes). The studies you cite are grouped in accordance with the stance or positions articulated by prominent scholars in the debate. In the sentence or two that follows your opening to the problem, you may want to move on to mention the particular topics, situations, or phenomena that will serve as the detailed object of investigation in the body of the study. The opening paragraph/s should become increasingly specific and detailed, leading to a very particular subject pointing to a clear and precise research question.

Research Question

Having set the stage with one or two opening paragraphs that introduce your essay, the next step is to present the research question that will guide your study. For a 20-page essay, ask only one or two carefully crafted

RESEARCH IN ACTION · Gail's story

For the final research paper in Gail's course in philosophy, the assignment required investigating codes of ethics. Since Gail had plans to apply to a master's program in philosophy with a concentration in bioethics, she began thinking about essay topics concerned with medical ethics, especially physicians' ethics.

Gail's research showed that the ancient *Oath* of Hippocrates, dated to about the fifth century BCE, has served as a template for a number of codes of conduct including the Declaration of Geneva. Over 95 per cent of medical students in North America swear an oath (commonly referred to as "the Hippocratic oath") at their graduation ceremony. Gail was surprised to learn, however, that hardly any medical schools asked students to recite the *Oath* verbatim. Most schools alter the wording of the *Oath* so that it conforms to contemporary ethics and values.

Gail decided that she would create an online digital essay that compared and contrasted the original text of the *Oath* with the modified oaths recited at three leading medical schools. Rather

research questions. These are generally one to three sentences in length. Theses over 40 pages should have no more than four questions, and this holds for longer studies as well. Undoubtedly, more questions need to be asked in a more extensive study, but in the Introduction, questions should be confined to those that serve as the focus of your investigation.

Questions that Can Be Answered

Try to make sure that the question/s you ask can be answered within the number of pages or screens that you have available for your assignment. Some questions call for only a short answer based on observable facts, so they do not provide the scope you need in order to develop an argument that displays your thinking and original ideas. Other questions require ten volumes for an appropriate response. Thus, your question should be of a depth and complexity that matches the parameters of your than merely citing sources in her footnotes, she decided to create links to the actual essays she was referencing. That way her readers could simply click on a link, find the quoted information in its original context, and read further if they chose. Gail also included images of Hippocrates as well as links to some of the earliest manuscripts of the *Oath*. For her comparative studies, she relied on the text analysis site Voyant Tools (www.voyant-tools.org) to carry out the analysis.

As she progressed with her inquiry, Gail could see that there were many variations on the *Oath*, yet almost every study retained some version of the "do no harm" principle from the original ancient text. She decided that this principle was the very essence of the physician's oath.

As she developed her study, Gail focused her analysis on the timelessness of the "do no harm" principle and its meaning for contemporary codes of medical ethics. She arranged to interview two physicians, two nurses, and two medical school students who were about to graduate. She asked them what the oath meant to them in the context of their careers, used her tablet to film the interviews, and then posted the digital essay on the university website.

assignment. Additionally, you may want to think about how your question lends itself to the use of digital technologies.

You will find that constructing a good question is no easy matter. If you are an undergraduate or master's student, you may not be expected to make an original contribution to the literature. Still, you will not earn extra points for reiterating a question that has already been dealt with many times in the literature such as "Does watching violent movies influence children to commit violent acts?" (research suggests that it does not, at least not directly). If your question is the product of extensive research dedicated to narrowing your topic, you should be able to offer some new take, angle, or approach to the issues, and this is an accomplishment in itself. For a digital essay in an art therapy class, for example, consider the following question: "Are there more violent images in the paintings of eighth-grade students who were exposed to films depicting trench warfare in the First World War as opposed to those who watched a Disney production?"

How to Formulate a Research Question

1. Find an interest in a broad subject area.
2. Narrow your interest to a plausible topic. Be specific. Name your topic:

    I am studying _____.
3. Use brainstorming techniques to develop a set of draft questions about your specific topic.
4. Suggest a question. Describe your work more precisely by adding an indirect question that specifies something about your topic that you do not know or fully understand, but want to learn. Your interests should guide this question. Try filling in the blanks:

    I am studying _____ because I want to find out who / what / when / where / whether / why / how / if _____ in order to understand how / why / what / whether _____.

Hypothesis

A good place to present the hypothesis is immediately following the research question. At the beginning of the investigation, the hypothesis is your best guess about what you will find in the end and why. A hypothesis is a theory, a premise, or a supposition. In other words, hypotheses predict the outcome of the research. A hypothesis is generally one to three sentences.

While not all studies demand a hypothesis—literary or thematic essays may not lend themselves to this element of an introduction—a solid hypothesis can serve as a placeholder for the thesis statement. It can guide your analysis and argument until you have conducted the literature review and analyzed the data and results and are able to formulate the thesis that will appear in the final study.

Often your research will uncover findings that are quite unlike the results you expected when you started out. Comparing the findings you expected initially with the actual results you obtained is one way to develop the Results or Findings section of the study.

Another good reason for having a hypothesis in the beginning is that if your research did not obtain the results you expected, a hypothesis will relieve you of having to go back and change the beginning of the study so that it tallies with your results.

Thesis Statement

The thesis statement outlines or summarizes the content of your piece in one to three sentences by setting forth either the central idea that you will develop or the conclusion that you will arrive at by the end of the study. Thus, the thesis statement provides an introductory answer to the research question.

An Early Thesis Statement

Your thesis should come as near to the beginning of your essay as possible. Why? It lets the reader know what your essay is about, and it reminds you of the main point of your study, or what you seek to accomplish. Placing the thesis after the hypothesis allows you to compare the results you anticipated with the conclusions that you arrived at after you actually carried out the investigation.

Studies that May Not Require a Thesis

Not all papers require a thesis statement. Some perfectly legitimate kinds of investigations do not involve the development of a central idea. For example, a paper for a journalism class might report on a situation such as the media response to a natural disaster like Hurricane Alberto in 2012. Likewise, an essay in physical geography might simply describe trends in weather patterns as measured by annual levels of rainfall in a particular region over a 10- to 20-year period. These sorts of descriptions contribute to the foundation of knowledge in the field and produce information that is of value. Yet studies such as these do not require a formal thesis.

Formulating the Thesis as a Later Research Stage

We underscore that while a thesis statement should come at the start of the essay, the actual formulation of the thesis statement cannot be accomplished until late in the writing process. Since the thesis introduces the conclusion, what you have found and the argument you will make need to emerge from the literature review, the analysis in the body of the study, and the findings that result from your investigation. Thus, the material you develop in your study provides the support for the thesis.

Crafting the Thesis Statement

If you have been developing all the parts of your essay and are still having difficulty formulating a thesis, go back over your notes and drafts. Ask yourself these questions:

1. What conclusions do the literature review, analysis, and results suggest?
2. What connections can I make?
3. Now that I have all my material together, what claims will this material support?
4. What thesis can I derive from my analysis of the literature and observations?

The Thesis: Delimited, Cohesive, and Precise

An excellent thesis statement is delimited, cohesive, and precise. First, it is delimited in the sense that its borders are clearly demarcated. As with the question (and again, the thesis statement is a kind of response to the question), many students fall into the trap of creating a thesis that is too large for the parameters of the assignment.

Delimiting the Thesis

A statement such as "Television advertisements frequently deceive viewers" is so general that it could be the subject of an entire book or a three-part documentary television series. Limiting the thesis makes clear the subject of the paper and the direction the argument will take in order to support that conclusion—for example, "Philco Pharmaceutical's 2013 television advertising campaign for FastDiet weight reduction pills withheld information about serious side effects that should have been disclosed to consumers."

Coherence

An excellent thesis is cohesive; it should express one main idea. If the thesis statement is not unified around a central idea but instead presents two or three different ideas, you will commit yourself to developing each of those parts separately, which may involve more writing and research than you can handle effectively. Here is an example:

> Low-income families in the Smiths Falls area have difficulty affording childcare and finding suitable housing, even when both parents work outside the home.

This statement commits you to supporting the fact that two people can be working and their combined income can still fall below the poverty level in this region of the country. You also have to show that the working poor frequently do not earn sufficient income to afford childcare in that area. And you have to provide evidence that affordable housing is in short supply.

Here is a more workable thesis:

> Data in a recently released report by the Ontario Ministry of Education indicates there is no affordable daycare in the Smiths Falls region for families with a combined annual income of less than $30,000.

In this case, the thesis has narrowed its focus to a combined annual income, the Smiths Falls region, and affordable childcare, so evidence concerning the available daycare facilities and their annual cost would be sufficient to support this claim.

Rigour and Precision

An excellent thesis is precise and rigorously stated. This means that the thesis can be interpreted in only one way. You should examine your thesis carefully to eliminate vagueness or ambiguity. The thesis, "In international politics, might makes right," may be an interesting turn of phrase, but what does it mean exactly? This sentence can be interpreted any number of ways. When writing your thesis statement, try to eliminate this sort of ambiguity.

A Response to the Question

Again, think of the thesis statement as your response to a problem or set of issues, the answer to the research question, the main point of the essay, or the conclusion of your study.

Try reading the question out loud and then immediately after that read the thesis out loud. Does the thesis seem to provide an adequate response to the question? If your Introduction includes a hypothesis, read the question, hypothesis, and thesis in sequence.

Statement of Significance

The statement of significance is a crucial component of every academic essay and is typically three sentences to several paragraphs in length. Right up front, your readers should be informed about why the study is important.

What is at stake in terms of the problems or issues being addressed in the study? To whom are these issues relevant? What might happen if nothing is done about this situation or problem? Do you anticipate things will proceed in a positive or negative direction? Why should we be concerned about these issues? What are the implications for individuals, groups, or society and culture as a whole? If the problems are ignored, what will happen? What is the likely impact? How is the specific case related to broader concerns? Providing a statement of significance lets your readers know why your study is important. Readers should never have to figure this out for themselves.

Purpose

Readers want to know why you are researching the topic you have chosen. What are your major objectives? What do you aim to achieve? What exactly will the study accomplish? What are your goals for this research? Think about the purpose of your inquiry and spell this out clearly for readers in one or two sentences.

The Purpose of the Thesis Is Demonstration—Not Proof

Keep in mind that the limitations of the thesis, capstone, or major research project are such that it is seldom possible to provide definitive proof of anything. Rather, the purpose of the inquiry might be to show, describe, assess, consider, examine, illustrate, or analyze. Are you having trouble formulating the goals of your study? Remember, in many cases, simply achieving a greater understanding of some phenomenon is a worthy goal.

Statement of Scope and Limitations

It is worthwhile stating the scope and limitations of your study explicitly in two to four sentences. How much territory will your essay cover? How big is the study?

Why include this statement? It is easy to criticize a study for the information that is not covered. However, if you state outright and up front what will be covered and what will not be dealt with in the study, it is difficult for readers to accuse you of leaving something out. What is beyond the purview of your investigation and why?

As examples, consider these two statements of scope and limitations:

This study examines changes in legislation concerning the pesticide DDT in southern Saskatchewan between 1967 and 1970.

This project uses information from the wills of three generations of the McCarthy family (1905–1940) of Vancouver as case studies that elucidate changing patterns of inheritance among middle class Canadians in the first half of the twentieth century.

In the first example, you could not be expected to discuss the use of the pesticide in the United States in the 1950s. In the second case, your readers might expect a paragraph or two explaining how the wills of the McCarthy family are representative of other estates during this time frame, but you would not be expected to discuss other wills in any length.

Preliminary Definitions

Many academic studies are improved with the addition of one or more definitions of the major terms employed in the question or thesis statement. These definitions may be five or six sentences, as necessary. For example, if you are researching "men's fashion as a semiotic system," you may want to spell out for your readers exactly how you will be using the words *fashion* and *system* in your study.

Researching and Creating Definitions

As we have emphasized before, you should create your own definitions rather than simply citing the *Oxford English Dictionary*.

This does not mean that you make up a definition. What it means is that you put together a definition in your own words that references other authors or practitioners who have provided similar definitions.

If you do use another author's definition, it should be the standard in the field. In addition, definitions should be brief and limited to those terms that are absolutely necessary for your project.

Assumptions

Try to make explicit any underlying assumptions that ground your investigation. Assumptions are generally one or two sentences to one paragraph in length. Consider this example: "The assumption in this study is that the plays credited to William Shakespeare were not written by Sir Francis Bacon."

Outline of the Argument

It is important that you provide guideposts for your readers so they know how you will be developing your study. These one to three paragraphs typically come at the end of the Introduction and before the Review of Literature. Here is an example:

> This study begins with an analysis of the arguments concerning a revolution in the distribution of power from men to women over the last half century. Next, I present evidence that shows how men still control the most important industries, occupy most of the places on the lists of the

richest Canadians, and continue to earn more money than women with similar education and skills. Then, I argue that while the limitation of male entitlements and the expansion of women's legal and economic rights have changed Canadian life, they have not produced a matriarchy. Indeed, I present evidence showing that the progress of women has sputtered to a halt over the last fifteen years. The study ends with suggestions for further research.

In a few sentences, the summary of the argument provides readers with the entire trajectory of the project that will be presented in the study to support the claims made in the thesis statement.

 FINAL CHECKLIST

- ○ Begin to envision the entire project and map out and start drafting all the components of the essay, bearing in mind the tools and techniques available to you.
- ○ Think about your title and subtitle. Continue to refine and polish them until you are ready to submit your final draft.
- ○ Describe the problem to be addressed in your study and contextualize the issues.
- ○ Begin with a statement that presents an overview and then narrow the lens of the inquiry.
- ○ Identify a gap in the literature, one or more unquestioned assumptions, existing biases, a missing piece of the puzzle, or a controversy or debate.
- ○ Group authors around the arguments they make, methods they employ, or positions they take.
- ○ Narrow the problem statement to a focused research question.
- ○ Provide the hypothesis in the study; describe how you will go about testing your hypothesis or theory.
- ○ Present the thesis that will be argued in the essay; concentrate on constructing a restricted, unified, and precise thesis statement.
- ○ Explain the reasons why your study is important and why your research is significant.

○ Offer a list of objectives.

○ Set forth the scope of your study (how big it is and what will be covered) and the limitations (what you will be leaving out and why).

○ Provide definitions for key concepts.

○ Identify underlying assumptions, both in your own work and in the literature.

○ Present a summary outline of the argument.

Chapter Summary

This chapter described the various components of an Introduction that most forms of scholarly writing have in common. We discussed the criteria by which excellence can be measured for the various components, with the view that if the parts of the essay are well formulated, the project as a whole will be outstanding. We also presented several examples that illustrate how you might think about integrating a more traditional academic essay with digital media. Again, we emphasized the importance of rewriting, of questioning assumptions, and of doing the kind of polishing that will create an excellent piece of work.

10

The Review of Literature

Chapter Outline

In this chapter we continue with the detailed description and explanation of the components of the digital essay. At this point, you have the big picture of your project in mind as you work to fill in all the pieces of the study. We suggest ways you might incorporate some of the digital media tools we discussed earlier. We present these elements in the order they typically appear in the final product rather than the order in which you might have to create them. We also provide an example you might model for your project. This chapter focuses primarily on the Review of Literature, and it also offers a preliminary discussion concerning the Methodology section of your study.

Review of Literature

The Review of Literature is a crucial component of your assignment and (in the hypothetical 7,000 word digital essay we are using as a rough guide) is generally 500 to 1,000 words or two to four pages in length. In a thesis or dissertation, the Review of Literature is typically a separate chapter. Though it is located after the Introduction, the literature review should be one of the first sections of the essay you undertake in order to get your research underway. It is difficult to write the Introduction, for example, without having a solid draft of the Review of Literature.

Revising the Proposal's Review of Literature

If you wrote a proposal, you developed a fairly good draft of the Review of Literature, which can now be revised for the final version that you submit. Through writing your proposal, you learned about the history of scholarship relative to your problem as well as the controversies on the leading edge of research in your area. The literature review also helped you to think about the method that might serve as the basis of the body of your study—including the way that you will be incorporating digital media into your project. At this stage, you should be taking the Review of Literature that you created for your proposal and refining it further to accommodate the amount of space you have for it within the total space available for the study—typically 15 to 20 per cent of the final essay.

Correlating the Review of Literature and the Analysis or Body Section

As you work with the elements of your study, we suggest you begin carefully correlating the main points of the Review of Literature with the material you are developing in the Analysis or Body section of your study. Every section of the literature review should be absolutely necessary to understand the Analysis or Body section of the essay. If you develop ideas in the literature review and do not use them to interpret your data and evidence, then they should be removed before you submit your final project.

Sections of the Review of Literature

The Review of Literature can be broken down into the following components to make it easier and more manageable to write this portion of your project:

- the introduction and explanation of why you selected these areas of literature to answer your question/s;
- two or more mini-essays covering the major fields of literature, with these mini-essays presenting the "state of the art" of knowledge concerning your question—as well as the digital technologies you will be using;
- effective transitions showing the links among the areas of literature you have chosen for your study;
- a summary of findings;
- an outline of criteria used in the analysis; and finally,
- a transition to the Methodology section.

The Review of Literature as a Critical Framework for the Analysis

A literature review is (1) a description and critique of the academic literature (i.e., the various books, chapters, articles, journals, and most often cited sources); and (2) an examination of what the academic literature reveals about the subject of your investigation. The Review of Literature is an exploration of one or more subject areas, which will provide a framework for research and an overview of the methods, tools, and criteria you need for your analysis and interpretation in the central sections of your paper. The methods you highlight when reviewing the work of other scholars in your literature review should include those that are used to analyze data in your field as well as the digital tools and techniques that you will employ in your study.

Purpose of the Review of Literature

Many students are not experts on their chosen topic when they start reading. The idea is that through the process of writing the literature review, you will develop an excellent working knowledge of the background to the problem and this will lead you to the most current research in the area. The purpose of your Review of Literature is to document both your research into the work of others and your thinking and critique of that research.

Information-Seeking Skills

In addition to expanding your understanding of your topic, writing a literature review allows you to demonstrate your information-seeking skills—you want to show that you are able to scan the literature efficiently and that you can identify and present a set of useful articles and books in an ordered format.

Organization of Information

The literature review also shows that you are able to sort through a welter of studies related to your problem and organize the best work in your area into carefully constructed explanations of what has gone before.

Critical Evaluation

Your literature review also highlights your critical appraisal skills. You want to show your reader that you are capable of applying principles of analysis to identify the most appropriate and valuable studies and to identify the faults, limitations, gaps, erroneous assumptions, and other issues in all the works that you cite.

Introduction to the Review of Literature: Rationale

The literature review opens with a paragraph that introduces the bodies of research studies that you will be relying on as evidence to respond to the hypotheses and to support the claims you make in your thesis statement. Your introduction also provides a rationale for the relevance of each area of literature to your specific study. It may also justify your use of particular digital tools and techniques for the research that will be discussed in the Methodology section of the essay.

Why Bring Together These Research Areas?

Why did you choose these two to three areas of research to respond to your question? Why are these areas of research more relevant and significant than other studies that might at first appear to have more claim to our attention with regard to the issues? How will you be fitting these bodies of literature together leading up to your description of the methodology in the next portion of the study?

Prioritization

It is also worthwhile saying a few words about why you have ordered the information in your presentation the way that you have. Why are you starting with one group of studies while another comes later in your presentation?

Though you do not have to answer every one of these questions in the introductory paragraph to your Review of Literature, these are the sorts of explanations that will help your readers understand the logic behind the choices you have made for your study—and show that you have good reasons for organizing and laying out your paper in the way that you have.

Sections of the Review of Literature

After the introductory paragraph/s, the parts of the review that follow set forth the research literature and assess the strengths and weaknesses of various arguments, claims, assumptions, views, and positions of the authors cited as well as the merits of the methods they use. Bear in mind your own research question as well as the claims (either explicit or implicit) in your thesis statement. The mistake many students make is to think of the review as a kind of annotated bibliography of the works referenced; these students move from one article or author to another, as though it were a list, and they describe or summarize the content of each of the studies. Unless there are only a few key studies in an area and they need to be treated in depth, describing one study after another almost never makes for an excellent Review of Literature.

Format

A good literature review can present information any number of ways. Sometimes a reviewer adopts a chronological sequence to present the history of thinking about a particular issue. More often, the reviewer (1) abstracts main principles, issues, ideas, and methods; (2) groups authors around positions or approaches; and then (3) assesses or weighs the strengths or weaknesses of the arguments or evidence presented by those authors who subscribe to a position or point of view.

Division into Mini-Essays

One way of making the writing more manageable is to think about the bodies of literature that you survey in the literature review as being divided into two to four mini-essays. Each mini-essay presents the material, reflects on it, weighs evidence, and evaluates the scholarship crucial to your research question/s.

As you create each of these sections, you will be attempting to find and make explicit the set of related assumptions or research paradigms that you will either problematize or draw upon for future sections of your study.

Bear in mind as well that each of the mini-essays or sections must transition into the subsequent section. Try as well to highlight points of relevance or connection between the material that comes before or goes after a particular section.

Goals

You should aim for your literature review to set forth the current state of knowledge about your problem and question, expose holes in the literature,

RESEARCH IN ACTION · Jacob's story

Jacob was hoping to use his thesis and capstone project to unite his studies in communication and media with his interests as a political science major. He decided he would like to examine cultural critiques with a view to uncovering why they seem to have had so little impact and why they have rarely resulted in positive change.

When Jacob was working on his proposal, he had created a blog to which he added images and drafts of his project. He also installed an aggregator and set up RSS feeds, so he automatically received notices of website content relevant to his research. Additionally, he signed on to the citation manager dashboard Mendeley and joined a number of social bookmarking sites including Academia.edu and ResearchGate.

In his proposal, Jacob had devoted one mini-essay of his Review of Literature to the reception of the model of the media developed by Edward S. Herman and Noam Chomsky in their book *Manufacturing Consent: The Political Economy of the Mass Media* ([1988] 2002).

Jacob refined and condensed this material in the proposal to create a succinct mini-essay for his final paper. Examining the reception of *Manufacturing Consent* involved looking back at how the Herman/ Chomsky propaganda model was taken up by readers and how it influenced scholarship (Comoforo 2010, 218–30).

The main point of Jacob's mini-essay was that scholars and the mainstream media either ignored the critique presented by Herman and Chomsky or they viewed it negatively.

Jacob's Draft Review

After introducing this mini-essay in the Review of Literature, Jacob pointed to one of the main issues:

Following the publication of *Manufacturing Consent* in 1988, the Herman/Chomsky propaganda model garnered scant attention from media and communication studies, the broader social sciences, or the media itself. Herman and Chomsky had in fact predicted that their arguments would be ignored.

Jacob then showed his own thinking by offering reasons for this state of affairs—in other words, he attributed causality:

> That both scholars and the mainstream media disregarded the Herman/Chomsky model is not unexpected, given that Herman and Chomsky's arguments were sharply critical of the media.

Then Jacob provided solid evidence for the near total absence of press coverage in the United Kingdom, and he extended those findings to the North American context:

> In 2004, *MediaLens* reported that since 1988 the propaganda model had been mentioned only once in *The Guardian*, while a media database search turned up just ten references in other British newspapers over that time period (MediaLens 2004). Results were similar for American and Canadian newspapers.

Jacob commented further on the gap in scholarship and went on to list the studies that took a negative view:

> What is more perplexing is the extent to which social scientists, who are often convinced that they are unbiased, have neglected the Herman/Chomsky propaganda model. The few studies that did mention the Herman/Chomsky model were overwhelmingly negative (Corner 2003; Eldridge 1993; Entman 1990a, 1990b; Golding and Murdock 1991; Goodwin 1994; Hallin 1994; LeFeber 1988; Lemann 1989; Nelson 1990; Schlesinger 1989; Schudson 1989; Sparks 2007).

Jacob's next statement weighed the evidence presented by those studies that reacted negatively to the arguments of Herman and Chomsky. Then, he offered his own critique of the criticisms of the propaganda model, pointing out that they offered almost no support for the arguments presented:

> It is significant that the majority of these commentators and scholars did not engage with the Herman/Chomsky model

Continued . . .

on its own terms; they attributed to it claims that Herman and Chomsky did not make, and they avoided the extensive evidence they marshalled, offering no alternative explanations for the phenomena.

In the statement that followed, Jacob evaluated the negative position toward the propaganda model as being very weak indeed:

> This flagrant avoidance of the facts is the opposite of good social science, wherein scholars objectively critique the assumptions, arguments, and conclusions of research presented by others in their disciplines.

Jacob went on to present the other side of the debate, listing those scholars who have taken the opposing view. He pointed out that while these studies support Herman and Chomsky's findings, they did not mention their writings explicitly. Notice how the sheer weight of this scholarship gives us, as readers, reason to suspect that the Herman/Chomsky propaganda model may not be inaccurate:

> A number of studies have presented evidence that supports the core hypotheses urged by Herman and Chomsky (Aronson 1990; Babe 2005; Boyd-Barrett 2004; Chomsky 1991; Gunn 1994; Hammond and Herman 2000; Herman and O'Sullivan 1989, 1991; Herring and Robinson 2003; Klaehn 2005; Lee and Solomon 1990; McMurtry 1998; Parenti 1986; Phillips 2007; Winter 1992, 1998, 2002; Winter and Klaehn 2005).

Jacob pointed to the silence concerning this relevant body of work and then went on to point out both a contradiction and a gap in the literature:

> As might be anticipated, however, these studies have also been ignored. Furthermore, although they did not use the Herman/Chomsky model, a number of scholars in the United Kingdom and North America agreed that the mass media has a tendency

to construct consent for elite preferences with respect to domestic and foreign policy issues (Altheide 2006; Andersen 2006; Bennett 1990; Carruthers 1995; Curtis 1984; Domhoff 1979; Entman 1991; Glasgow University Media Group 1985; Greenslade 2003; Hallin 1986; Hollingsworth 1986; Knightley 2003; Lashmar and Oliver 1998; Mermin 1999; Miliband 1969; Miller 2004; Philo and McLaughlin 1993; Zaller and Chui 1996). While the Herman/Chomsky model has been applied within the American context, and while Edwards and Cromwell (2005) and Miller (in Klaehn 2006) have alluded to its potential to explain certain aspects of the media in other countries, few studies have tried to test it systematically within the Canadian context.

Notice how Jacob acknowledged the study that contested the applicability of the propaganda model to other media systems—he did not ignore this research that went against the argument he was making—even as he gave us reason to suspect that this study, too, may be inaccurate or biased.

Jacob thereby paved the way to his own analysis of the applicability of the Herman/Chomsky model to the Canadian media scene and to a further consideration of why critical studies are often poorly received by those with a stake in the status quo:

Indeed, one critic questioned whether it could even "be applied in countries with very different media systems and polit- ical structures" (Corner 2003, 367). Nevertheless, studies by Doherty (2005) and Mullen (2010) have provided evidence that suggests the propaganda model may indeed be applicable to the media in other countries.

After that, Jacob transitioned to the next mini-essay:

The reception of Herman and Chomsky's propaganda model is not unique. Several other critical studies in other disciplines have met a similar fate.

pinpoint problems or controversies, identify the crux of the debates, expose unquestioned assumptions, and underscore the various ways of approaching the issues. This will help situate your research within the discussion that is currently taking place among the most recognized authorities.

A related goal is to identify a place for your essay within the debate by showing how your work extends existing knowledge and makes an original contribution by bringing something new to the table.

The Review of Literature as Critical Evaluation

Most importantly, the literature review goes far beyond merely describing the views of the authors you reference by providing a critique of previous studies. This last point is so important it bears repeating. Your goal in the review is not to describe the work of others but to organize their research and critique the views they expound and the positions they take.

What are the strengths and weaknesses of the arguments presented by authorities? How well do they line up with the evidence? Do they emphasize some facts while ignoring others? What are the assumptions they make? How do studies fall within a particular research tradition and therefore demonstrate both the positive and negative features of a particular school of thought?

If by the end of the Review of Literature you can show that your study offers a more comprehensive explanation of the evidence, then you have provided your reader with a good reason for accepting your thesis. Your central aim is to critically examine the literature with an eye to challenging assumptions even as you cite evidence in support of your own views.

Review Summary: Criteria for the Analysis

The finale of the literature review is a short outline of the main points uncovered in your survey of the literature. This outline underscores the key themes, issues, ideas, questions, methods, or approaches that will direct the Analysis or Body section of your digital essay. Thus, your Review of Literature should help you identify the main devices and tools that you will use in the Methodology section of the study, as well as the criteria you will apply to the analysis and interpretation of the data and other evidence you present in the Analysis or Body section of your essay.

Research Problems as Puzzles

One way to view the processes of conducting research and composing the Review of Literature is to think of your problem as analogous to assembling a jigsaw puzzle—there are many pieces missing and some pieces that do not belong. You examine the pieces that you have, discard the ones that do not seem to fit, attempt to determine how the missing pieces might look, and then try to fit them all together to form a unified construct.

To assemble the puzzle, the vision of the completed picture is crucial. That is why the puzzle typically comes with a photo of the fully assembled picture on the box.

Paradigms in Research

In jigsaw puzzles and in research, the total picture or vision of the field serves as a **paradigm**—from the Greek word *paradeigma*, meaning pattern, exemplar, or to exhibit by setting side by side. The big picture provides a context and a conceptual frame that guides the sorting and weighing of pieces—of the jigsaw or evidence—and determines the ways in which parts are connected, providing clues about how whole sections of the puzzle come together.

In research, a paradigm is the idea that a theory, method, or even a specific case serves as a model for examining other things that appear to be of the same type. In other words, paradigms are crucial ideas, constructs, models, or patterns that guide and shape research.

With your research, you are attempting to piece together a kind of puzzle to find a solution to a problem or to resolve an issue even though you do not have the benefit of any depiction of the whole. You must rely on theories of the big picture and methods of investigation that have been built up over years or even centuries through the accumulated contributions of many researchers—hence the convention of citing previous authorities.

Evidence and the Research Paradigm

Disagreements among the scholars you review will often stem from different perspectives on the big picture or on entirely different visions of the problem. You should be on the lookout for the kinds of evidence that scholars in your field have a hard time fitting into their paradigms. Often this problematic evidence can be found in critiques of an account offered by scholars with competing views. Also, watch for evidence related to the problem that no previous researcher has mentioned.

Examining All the Evidence

Evidence that does not fit into the current paradigms is often not observed by researchers, as studies have shown (Kuhn 1970). The crucial feature of paradigmatic theories and methods is that they come to dominate research so completely that gaps in the overall picture are not recognized and evidence that does not cohere with the pattern is either not seen as significant, or it is not seen at all!

More crucially still, predominating paradigms have such a hold over the minds of scholars that sometimes even facts are rejected if they do not fit into prevailing constructs (Kuhn 1970, 24).

Thomas Kuhn, philosopher of science, argues that the truly creative work involves overturning existing paradigms and creating a new one that brings all the available evidence together into a unified theory (1970). Sir Isaac Newton, for example, created the paradigm known as Newtonian physics or Newtonian mechanics, which became the dominant scientific view of the universe for the next three hundred years. Newton demonstrated that the motions of objects on Earth and of celestial bodies follow the same set of natural laws, thereby providing a unified explanation of phenomena and laying to rest once and for all the notion that the sun circled the earth, rather than the other way around.

Kuhn argues that as a new paradigm is investigated more fully, more and more anomalies are identified and gaps in the picture are filled. For a time, reconciling anomalous facts comes to preoccupy the best researchers in a paradigm until eventually, it is overthrown and a new paradigm becomes the focus of research and debate.

Thus Albert Einstein changed the paradigm of Newtonian mechanics by demonstrating that it could not account for the laws of electromagnetic fields. His special theory of relativity provided an explanation for irregular phenomena that did not fit with Newton's theory. Later, he found that his principle of relativity applied to gravitational fields as well; he developed his general theory of relativity, and Einsteinian physics supplanted Newtonian physics as the dominant paradigm in science.

Today, physicists are hard at work identifying anomalies in Einstein's theory that they can use to overthrow his paradigm and replace it with a unified theory.

The Superior Account

How do researchers and professors distinguish a superior account from other accounts that attempt to explain the same evidence? Kuhn offered this rule: the more evidence for which an interpretation can account, the greater its explanatory value relative to alternative interpretations of the evidence proposed by others.

Even if you are a beginning researcher, you can examine all of the evidence, try to step outside current research paradigms, think about what might be missing, trust your own judgment, and try to come up with an account that explains more of the evidence than the ones that are currently offered in the literature.

Remember, the strength of any one theory of interpretation depends on how well its central ideas can be reconciled with all the available evidence. This includes, first of all, the material that others have deemed most significant; second, the evidence that exists but which other researchers did not highlight as relevant or include in their rendering of the total picture; and third, how well the theory accounts for inconsistencies and anomalies that cannot be explained by other accounts.

One test of the power of a theory or method is its ability to expose the inadequacies of other perspectives. A superior theory holds out the potential for extending knowledge of the data that it reveals as significant, for increasing the extent of the match between the data and the theory's predictions, and for the further articulation of the theory itself.

Thus Newton concentrated on explaining why his theory provided a more comprehensive yet simpler and more elegant explanation of the phenomena than the competing view. When Einstein wanted to make his mark in the discipline of physics, he focused on developing an account of phenomena that could not be explained by way of Newtonian theory.

Lessons from Newton and Einstein

What if you are not yet a researcher of Newton's or Einstein's caliber? The lesson that a junior researcher can take away from the examples of Newton and Einstein is that in pursuing your research and developing and polishing your Review of Literature, you should be on the lookout for gaps, anomalies, or contradictions in previous research.

Discovering anomalies, irregularities, or inconsistencies is an excellent way to make a contribution to your field. You need not overturn an entire theory. At the student level, it is enough to simply find a piece of evidence that may not fit into the current paradigm, point to an assumption that has not been questioned, or highlight a piece of evidence or an example that may not have been deemed relevant by previous researchers. Using a new digital tool or technique on a long-standing problem may help to uncover new evidence that was not noticed previously. Even the most accomplished professional researchers in your discipline may not have recognized gaps—certain pieces of the puzzle that are missing. Or they may have ignored or downplayed evidence that is relevant to the problem. Or greater weight than is warranted may have been assigned to a piece of evidence. Text analysis tools may bring to light new correlations that were not apparent simply through close reading. Computational and statistical methods can be used to demonstrate that previous uses of evidence are not valid.

Arena of Opportunity

Using your literature review and new digital techniques to help you identify relevant evidence or critique existing uses of evidence is an arena of opportunity in a discipline. As you compose your Review of Literature—indeed, at every stage of creating your project—keep your eyes open for assumptions that create blind spots or facts that do not fit into the arguments offered by the authorities.

···FINAL CHECKLIST···

○ Start with the Review of Literature you worked up for your proposal and begin to revise with the total project—or big picture—in mind.

○ Concentrate on tightening the literature review you created for the proposal so that it includes only the evidence that is vital to your argument.

○ Explain the rationale for your selection of the fields of research you are highlighting and the logic behind their inclusion in your study.

○ Break down the literature review into several mini-sections. To make your tasks more manageable, focus on polishing these shorter components.

○ As you refine the literature review and hone your critique, continually ask yourself, "Why is this important to my argument?"

○ To group authors around various positions, ask yourself the following questions: "What are the principles, theories, or positions these studies have in common? Which studies take the opposite approach? Are there studies that occupy the middle ground between these two extremes?"

○ What are the major paradigms that dominate your discipline? Can you organize your Review of Literature around the major or competing paradigms and the reasons offered for accepting one or the other by the proponents? What are the counterarguments to the arguments?

○ What kinds of evidence do authorities cite to support their positions? Does the evidence add up to a compelling case? What are the strengths and weaknesses of the interpretations?

○ Summarize the findings from the Review of Literature so that you clearly establish the criteria and background to the methods you will use for your research.

Chapter Summary

This chapter presented an in-depth description and explanation of a major component of the digital essay, the Review of Literature section. An extended example showed how to go about incorporating digital research and how to produce a critical analysis. We also explained the role of paradigms in research and how finding evidence that has been overlooked or does not mesh with current accounts is one way to make a contribution to research. In the next chapter, we move on to the Methodology section of the paper and describe a number of discipline-specific methods to help you formulate your research design.

Methods, Methodology, and Digital Media

Chapter Outline

Chapters Eleven and Twelve concentrate on the most commonly used research methods in various disciplines and on creating the Methodology section of the study. In this chapter, we focus on the methods you select for your project and on how the media you choose reinforce your academic research. The section of a study that explains the methodology, including how new media and technologies will be incorporated into the investigation, follows the Review of Literature and builds on its findings. A checklist helps with the sequencing of steps for the development of the Methodology section.

The Methodology Section

The Methodology section continues with the critique of the theories and methods set forth in the summary of findings at the end of the Review of Literature. This summary provides the logic and rationale for the study and explains and justifies the method you have selected for your analysis. In picking up where the literature review leaves off, the Methodology section of the study explains the approach so that your research study can be duplicated and results verified or falsified. The Methodology section generally ranges from one or two paragraphs (in a 7,000 word study) to one chapter in length (in a thesis or dissertation).

Relationship among Disciplines, Theories, Methods, and Methodologies

Many scholars argue that the divisions that separate the disciplines indicate that all research is discipline-specific and theory-driven (Mitchell 1994).

The critique of the method therefore takes into account the theory— the set of interrelated principles that explain some thing, situation, or phenomenon that is grounded on general laws or rules. The Methodology section also provides an account of how the theory and methods intersect in your discipline/s.

Remember that a method is a research technique or tool for gathering evidence or to analyze or test phenomena. A methodology goes beyond a description of tools and techniques to question and critique the assumptions, premises, principles, comprehensiveness, or unity of the method itself.

Methodological issues emerge from the interaction among theories, forms of knowledge, social practices, and research methods. New insights about methods can make important contributions that lead to improved research practices by fostering consistency among underlying suppositions, concepts, and knowledge production activities (Young 2010, 122).

Purpose of the Methodology Section

The purpose of the Methodology section or chapter of your study is to explain how you will conduct the investigation so that other researchers will have sufficient information to replicate your study. The chapter should begin with a paragraph that explains the purpose of the study in terms of how the major components of the project operate together to respond to the research questions. The Methodology section may include the following components:

- an introduction with a statement of the purpose of the methods;
- a defense of the choice of method in comparison with alternative approaches;
- a detailed account of the research design including digital media;
- research involving human participants; and
- a concluding summary.

Suitability of Method

Following the paragraph outlining the purpose, the next paragraph in your Methodology section should justify the choice of the method/s you employ in your investigation by comparing and contrasting them with other possible approaches and explaining why those alternatives are not suitable for your project.

This paragraph sets forth a logical research design that is aligned with the purpose of the study.

Research Design

Scholars choose methods in order to produce particular types of outcomes (e.g., observation, description, persuasion, classification, measurement, control, or prediction). Having set forth the purpose and methods and critiqued the approaches taken by your intellectual predecessors, you will explain in the next paragraphs how you plan to go about constructing the research design.

The research design involves the steps you use to find an answer to the research question and includes the following stages:

- collection of data;
- analysis of findings;
- interpretation of evidence;
- summary of results; and
- drawing significant conclusions.

Designing the Research Method

A number of factors need to be taken into consideration when selecting a research method and creating the research design.

Recent Approaches

First, what is your assessment of the current knowledge concerning methods? What recent work has been done? How did it stack up? Can you try to verify or falsify the results obtained by a previous researcher? Are there aspects of earlier studies that require rethinking?

Original Contribution to Knowledge

In all cases, the ideal is for a research study to make an original contribution to knowledge. Even when assignments emphasize only a competent assessment and critique of prior studies—your professor may not expect a completely original contribution to knowledge—you should try to provide some new angle or approach to the material that represents your original insights. ◉))

Research Costs

Be aware of the costs of the research in terms of money, time, computer resources, and even the emotional involvement required. You may want to make a short animated film to illustrate your ideas, but you will not be able to produce a quality product if you have limited access to the necessary equipment; have rarely used a camera; have no budget for lighting, equipment, or crew; or have left the assignment to the night before it is due. Make sure the costs of your research are aligned with your resources.

Ethical Issues: Research Involving Human Participants

Every university has an ethics review board that offers a public **statement of ethics concerning research on human participants.** ◉)) If your research involves human participants in any way, you will need to submit a document to the university outlining your project and the methods you will employ—for example, survey questions, face-to-face interviews, photographing or videotaping interviewees, or otherwise making contact with individuals who are involved with your research as primary sources.

Institutional Review Board

Your university's Institutional Review Board vets every program of research involving human participants. Know the policies regarding human subjects as early as possible. Your institution will have these policies and the forms that need to be submitted for approval of your project posted on the Office of Research website.

Permissions

To be able to fill in the forms, the Methodology section (including an explanation of the digital media you will be using) will have to be solidly formulated. Typically, you will need to have formulated the questions you will ask your participants in personal interviews or in surveys. You will also need to explain your plans for dealing with issues such as respondents' right to privacy, the importance of informed consent, and possible implications for participants, as well as confidentiality of information, data access, and data storage. Know the procedure at your institution if your work involves any sort of interaction with people. Allow extra time for permissions.

No Method Is Perfect

Every method is open to criticism. As the researcher, it is up to you to determine which method can produce the best results. Having reviewed the literature relevant to your problem, you should be familiar with the strengths and weaknesses of different approaches and understand their potential applicability to your research project.

Research Goals

Set specific goals for yourself and adopt strategies for attaining them. Monitor your performance for signs of progress. Manage your use of time efficiently. Evaluate your method. And try to attribute causation to results. To be an effective researcher, you will need to be conscientious and self-reflective.

Methods and Data

Your research design should take into account the possibility that there may be flaws in your data selection or in your own thinking about the material you gather. Remember that the paradigm structures the research problem by providing implicit rules regarding the issues that are relevant. The paradigm also determines how to proceed with the analysis and the choice of the analytical tools used to address research questions. Continually question the theoretical frameworks, paradigms, and methods as you conduct the investigation.

Anticipating Problems

How can you think outside the box, recognize assumptions, anticipate problems, and budget extra time? Academic research always takes much longer than you think is possible. Technological problems always occur: if you are presenting your methodology to others via a PowerPoint presentation, your computer will not connect with the equipment at the site of the lecture; if you are relying on an online survey, a prankster will log in repeatedly and skew your results. Be prepared for problems that will hamper your progress and factor in time to compensate.

Location and Participants

The Methodology of the study section explains the data sample. Mention the geographic location where your study will be conducted. Describe as well the number of participants and their demographics in your study and provide the justification for the sample you selected. Discuss the number of participants and/or the sample relative to the study's purpose.

Instruments

Explain the tools or instruments as well as the techniques and procedures that you will use to collect the data. Data collection tools may use an existing instrument or you may create them. If you created the questions, explain the process you used to formulate them and justify your choices. If you decide to use an existing tool, briefly describe the background including who created it and the measures that were used.

If the method includes interviews, provide an interview protocol that is likely to result in a regular process of data collection across all the interviews you conduct.

Note that interview questions are typically placed in the Appendix rather than in the Methodology section.

Data Collection

Describe and explain when and how you will collect the data. This description may include an itemized list of material you have included in the appendixes, such as the permission from your university's Institutional Review Board, the questions, and the consent forms. It will also describe the procedures you will use to collect the data.

Discipline-Specific Methods

Below, we outline a number of examples of the most commonly used research methods in the disciplines. The list is not exhaustive. It is of course possible to apply many of these methods to more than one discipline. For example, ethnography is pertinent to such disciplines as anthropology, sociology, and education; content analysis can be used in communication, linguistics, literature, and nursing; controlled experiments can be employed in biology, chemistry, and physics, as well as in psychology; participant observation can be used in anthropology and education; field research can be the main data collection method in sociology, political science, and education research; and interviews are useful in psychology, occupational therapy, political science, and sociology.

Many disciplines use similar methods, so the examples listed below under a specific field may be exactly what you need for your particular research design even if you are working in another discipline altogether.

Anthropology

To gather information about the social world, the field of anthropology employs methods that involve direct observation of individuals or groups of people in their natural settings. The main task is to discern regularities in the behaviours of people as they perform the roles that are part of their social and cultural environment. This typically requires observers to become members of the communities they study.

Participant Observation

Participant observation is useful for understanding how activities and interactions within a setting or group give meaning to beliefs, values, or behaviours. The approach involves not just observation but note taking or recording.

While capturing people on video or cell phone without their knowledge seems an obvious way to carry out this sort of research, surreptitious study of human beings is not ethical. As you carry out your participant observation, try to avoid summarizing or generalizing; descriptions should be as factual as possible to allow for multiple interpretations and inferences about cultural meanings. The anthropologist Clifford Geertz called the approach "thick description."

Participant observation is relevant to many disciplines such as psychology, nursing, sociology, linguistics, social work, and business management.

Ethnography

Ethnography is an established method of participant observation that involves field research; it has as its aim a full depiction of the characteristics of a group or population. Ethnographic research entails describing a population's culture or way of life as a distinct point of view.

A key assumption is that every person is a reflection of his or her culture—all their gestures, displays, and symbols have some implicit meaning for others in that culture or group. The goal of ethnographic research is to tell the whole story of the daily life of this group and to identify the cultural meanings and beliefs that members attach to activities and behaviours.

Common characteristics and even culture are not limited to ethnic groups. Ethnographic approaches are useful for the study of the culture of organizations, programs, and groups of people with common social problems such as disabilities, family situations, or addictions.

Digital Ethnography

Digital ethnography refers to the application of new technologies to the process of ethnography. More specifically, digital ethnography describes the process and methodology of doing ethnographic research in a digital space.

If you keep track of users and assess their experiences using online surveys, polls, and other research instruments, you are using digital ethnographic methods. The digital field site might be a text, video, or image; it may contain social relations and behaviour patterns across many countries or cities; it may be composed around a single belief or attitude; or it can be a network of many different belief patterns, social customs, and actions.

Although digital ethnography is a relatively new area of research, its epistemology remains much the same as when ethnographic research was carried out by anthropologists in print culture. Good ethnography effectively communicates a social story, drawing the audience into the daily lives of its participants. With the introduction of new technologies, the stories remain. What has changed is the equipment and methods used to capture those stories and the ways those stories are told.

Ethnographic research in digital space examines the same relationships as in traditional studies: kinship, proximal relations, tool use, culture, language, customs, geography, philosophical beliefs, and patterns of behaviour in work, play, intimacy, and social class. Similar to traditional anthropologists, the first concern of digital ethnographers is to locate the field site and learn the language of the participants. For example, large online networks such as Facebook and Twitter have their own subgroups, including those that use languages other than English.

Whereas traditional anthropologists travel to another geographical location to pursue their research, digital ethnographers use the Internet to locate the field site. In some cases, the field site may be a mental construct created by a group of geographically distributed nodes on an information network.

Tools for Digital Ethnography

A digital ethnographer must have a set of tools for understanding and recording the digital space such as screen-capture software, website archiving tools, servers, blogs, and content management systems (the equivalent of the audio recorder and journal). To date, there are no groundbreaking works that collect and describe ethnographic or anthropological methods for digital researchers. But for able anthropologists, it will be easy to apply more traditional methods to the digital space. Different types of data (e.g., surveys, focus groups, or web server data logs) can provide different angles that can inform the research.

A number of tools can be effectively used in digital ethnography. Webcams and video conferencing provide accurate documentation of research participants and enable the recording of interviews and research sites.

Web questionnaires enable large-scale multi-site surveys of participants in different countries. E-mail interviews and focus groups are useful for gathering streams of information from otherwise inaccessible respondents.

Creating Custom Tools

You might consider working with programmers to create ways of locating and determining communication patterns in digital fields and to build custom tools for research. Web server data logs are a great vault of objective data such as entry/exit pages and the number and length of visits. You can analyze users' behaviour and comments, examine website traffic, or be involved in discussions with the users you are studying.

On the Internet, all user actions are automatically documented. An IP address is recorded every time a file or piece of information is requested from a server or sent to one. IP addresses can be traced to an individual machine. For online services that require a login, users' actions can be recorded and traced to that user.

Biology

The methods used in biology are different from those of sciences such as physics and chemistry. Typical biological concepts are more qualitative than those of the so-called hard sciences. Concepts such as life, organ, cell, or perception have no counterpart in physics or chemistry. At the same time, much of the research in biology is carried out by way of the application of chemistry and physics to living organisms.

Comparative Analysis

Like many other disciplines, biology and related fields often make use of techniques of comparative analysis. As an example, in evolutionary

RESEARCH IN ACTION · Massi's story

Massi's thesis and capstone project in the Media and Cultural Studies department at her university focused on the history of the Atlantic slave trade in the nineteenth century. Her interest had been sparked by the story that was passed down through generations of her family. Her parents told her that she had been named after her great-great-great-grandmother Massi, who was captured in Africa and forced onto a slave ship. Her ancestor survived the Atlantic crossing and was rescued and freed when the ship reached port in the Caribbean.

Massi discovered the African Origins Portal online database at www.african-origins.org, which lists thousands of records of Africans rescued from slave ships between 1808 and 1862. She found that slave traders typically kept good records. She also found accurate documentation of slaves who were released from a number of ships that reached Cuba. Several of the women were named Massi. Excited at the possibility that one of these women was her ancestor, she began tracing her family history, beginning with her parents and grandparents, and going back as far as possible through sites that provide online records of public documents such as Ancestry.com.

biology one or more features are compared across different species. For this sort of comparative work, you would have uncovered the criteria through your literature review, listed these features at the end of that section, and in the Methodology section, indicated that they will serve as the basis of the comparative analysis.

Digital tools can be used to aid examination and comparison of large samples and to monitor populations over time.

Business and Marketing

In the field of business, methods often draw upon complex economic models and detailed financial data for planning processes. In marketing, surveys and focus groups are widely used to identify preferences, as well as the effects of marketing campaigns.

She also focused her research on the larger cultural history of the slave trade and sugar plantations in the Caribbean as the context for her own family history.

Through the African Origins site, Massi learned that in the nineteenth century, there were no written African languages. The records on the site list the phonetic pronunciation along with an audio recording of how the African names of released slaves were documented, based on English pronunciations. Massi carried out an online search to identify professors with knowledge of African languages. She found one in the Linguistics department at her university. He listened to the names, identified the linguistic origins of the name, and identified Angola and the Congo as possible geographic regions from which Massi's relative had been forced to migrate.

For her Methodology section, Massi explained her genealogical research methods, and for the research design, she stated that she was using geography and geospatial web technologies to create a diagram of the various tribes and locations of the African linguistic groups that the professor had described to her. Massi consolidated her evidence through hyperlinks in her digital essay.

Focus Groups

Focus groups are useful when multiple viewpoints or responses are needed on a specific topic or issue. The value of the focus group is that many different responses can be obtained in a shorter period of time than would be possible by conducting individual interviews. That said, the principles that apply to individual interviews also apply to focus groups, including the use of open-ended questions and the concentration on listening and learning from the participants.

Digital Marketing Studies

Marketing studies offer a number of opportunities to make use of digital media such as online surveys, folksonomies, or even geotagging to identify local, national, or international markets.

Chemistry

Chemistry relies heavily on experimentation. Experimental methods are commonly used to determine causal relationships or to quantify the magnitude of the response of a variable.

Experimental Method

Scientific experimentation aims to determine the nature of the relationship between independent and dependent variables. Typically, one or more variables are manipulated, and the outcome or effect of that manipulation on other variables is observed. Often, a goal of an experimental design is to provide a measure of variability within a system and a check for sources of error. Thus, it is important that you understand which aspects of the experiment you are manipulating and to monitor them carefully in order to determine the impacts of actions.

Communication and Mass Media

The study of communication and mass media is approached through a number of methods including content analysis, controlled experiments, surveys, and observations, all of which can be conducted online with minor modifications of traditional features.

The experimental method (see Chemistry above) is one of the most commonly used methods. For example, one group of participants might be exposed to a particular advertisement and their reactions tested in comparison to the reactions of another group of participants who are not exposed to that particular content.

Surveys

Many survey studies use questionnaires that incorporate measures of media exposure (such as viewing television violence); this is a quantitative approach wherein the results are expressed as a series of correlations. Digital tools can be used to help you create your survey, and digital techniques can also be used to distribute and analyze the results.

Content Analysis

Content analysis is a technique for gathering and analyzing the content of speeches, texts, images, and other media. The content can be words, sentences, paragraphs, pictures, or arguments, and the content analysis can be either quantitative or qualitative.

Quantitative content analysis is used widely in mass communication as a way to count manifest textual elements. For example, content analyses may track the number of times specific words are mentioned or the regularity of the appearance of particular concepts. Images may be analyzed as "visual texts." Online digital text analysis portals such as TAPOR lend themselves to this sort of research.

There are some drawbacks to digital quantitative analyses. The approach has been criticized for missing syntactical and semantic information embedded in a text. Further, quantitative content analysis is deductive, and seeks to test hypotheses or address questions generated from theories or previous empirical research. If you decide to use this approach, try to select data through random sampling or other probabilistic methods to ensure that the statistical inferences you make are valid.

Qualitative content analysis, by contrast, is a method used to explore the meanings of messages. Data samples for qualitative content analyses usually consist of purposively selected texts, which inform the research questions under investigation. Whereas quantitative methods use computational approaches, qualitative studies seek to identify the specific themes that illustrate the range of the meanings of phenomena under investigation, rather than the statistical significance of the occurrence of words, sentences, or concepts.

Qualitative content analysis is mainly inductive (proceeding from a particular case to more general principles) and grounds the examination of topics, themes, and the inferences (implications or extrapolations) drawn from the data. If you decide to use qualitative content analysis, you will likely be condensing raw data into categories or themes based on your inferences and interpretations.

You will find that themes and categories emerge from the data through your own careful examination and comparison of the material. Often, though not always, you will find hints of these themes and categories in your sources as you put together the Review of Literature.

Combining Quantitative and Qualitative Approaches

Quantitative and qualitative approaches are not mutually exclusive and are frequently used in combination. In both, you will need to create a coding scheme, typically using basic terms such as frequency (amount of content), frames (how information is depicted), and space (in time as in the case of television or radio, or in centimetres as in the case of newspapers).

Cinema, Media Studies, Literature, and Cultural Studies

Hermeneutic, textual, feminist, psychoanalytic, arts-based, semiotic, or narrative analyses are among the methods commonly employed in cinema and literary studies. Film and media theory also incorporate some critical theories and methods, such as Marxist and feminist theories.

Critical Discourse Analysis

Critical discourse analysis is an approach that seeks to uncover the relationships between language use, power, and ideology by observing and tracking the regularity of particular events or sequences in the discourse.

You will need to divide your text into smaller categories (paragraphs, sentences, or words) to identify the following:

- instances of themes such as dominance and submission (as found in feminism and post-colonial studies);
- the handling of questions; or
- the assignment of roles in terms of race, gender, power, or age (as found in cultural studies or rhetorical analyses).

The notion of context is also crucial for critical discourse analysis, since this approach explicitly includes social, psychological, political, and ideological aspects. Post-structuralist approaches emphasize the openness as well as the variability or differences between studies in the estimates of effects of the text (i.e., heterogeneity), the way the text is embedded in history, and its political and ideological dimensions.

For instance, Continental philosophers such as Michel Foucault describe how texts and discourses are embedded in power, and feminists describe how patriarchy and subordination are inscribed in texts. Discourse analysis could employ a combination of digital computational techniques and more qualitative approaches to study rhetorical patterns in texts.

 FINAL CHECKLIST

- ○ Choose the methodology and the digital techniques you will employ in your study.
- ○ If your research will involve human participants, check with the research office at your university, contact your professors to let them know how you plan to proceed with your project, fill in the forms, obtain required signatures, and submit the document for approval.

○ Determine whether your research can be conducted online through the use of surveys or focus groups.

○ As you write the Methodology section, try to show how your project will (1) fill in the gaps in our knowledge about the method, (2) test assumptions, (3) challenge received views, or (4) critique problems and issues with the method.

Chapter Summary

This chapter focused on the components of the Methodology section and on the research methods specific to various disciplines. After completing the Review of Literature and a preliminary assessment of the research design, we explained how to identify the method/s you will employ in your study and how to document your incorporation of new media and technologies into your scholarly work. In so doing, we recommend that you look at traditional methods in light of the resources and tools we described in Chapters Three through Five. We suggested that you clarify the rationale for your project and explain how the media you select reinforce your academic research.

12

Methodology and the Project as a Whole

Chapter Outline

Chapter Twelve continues the discussion of the Methodology section as well as the research methods typically used in various disciplines. This chapter focuses on the methods you select for your project and on how the technologies you choose reinforce your academic research. We explain how the Methodology connects to other sections of the investigation and how to work simultaneously on the different pieces that make up the overall project.

Building Connections among the Sections of the Study

As you begin working on the Analysis or Body of the study, you will find that careful work on the Review of Literature and Methodology will bear fruit. These sections set forth and highlighted the prospects and challenges at the leading edge of inquiry in your discipline; the theories, methods, controversies, and debates put forward by scholars on all sides of an issue; the assumptions that scholars in the field share in common; the problems with the various arguments; and the gaps in the research. You should also have been able to establish the criteria that will now serve as the focus of your analysis in the sections that follow.

For example, if you are assessing candidates for prime minister or president in your assignment in political science, an outcome of the literature review might have been the criteria of charisma, background, and experience. These criteria then become the centre of the Methodology section as you explain how you will go about testing them through the methods you adopt for your study. These same criteria would then be employed in the Analysis or Body of your study as the basis for a comparative analysis of different leaders.

If you are comparing and contrasting proposals for landscape designs for neighbourhood parks for your studio class in landscape architecture and urban planning, you might use the criteria of usability, cost, and maintenance identified in the literature review.

For a study in zoology, you could decide to analyze species based on the criteria of structure, classification, and habits. The point is, competent literature reviews are connected to the Methodology section. And both set the stage for the writing that follows, forming the program for the Analysis or Body of the study, especially, but also focusing the sections of your study that set forth the Results or Findings and Conclusions.

Methods

This section picks up where Chapter Eleven left off; we continue with the outline of research methods used in various disciplines. These are some, though by no means all, of the approaches that are used.

Economics

The discipline of economics makes use of sophisticated mathematical and computational methods. Mathematical models are used to replicate systems through simplification in order to perform an experiment that cannot be done in the real world; to assemble several known ideas into a coherent whole; and to build and test hypotheses. Modelling involves developing conceptual or computer-based representations of systems to try to make predictions about how economic systems in the real world might change in the future. While modelling cannot predict exact outcomes, it can help you see the range of possibilities that a given set of changes might entail. Modelling can be combined with other research methods; for example, you might incorporate modelling into experimental, descriptive, or comparative studies.

Macroeconomics relies heavily on dynamic, general equilibrium models and makes use of formal methods of probability-based inference. Microeconomics, on the other hand, relies on controlled experiments to understand issues such as risk aversion, how people assess risks, and so forth.

Geography

Methods employed in geography often rely on the systematic observation and cataloguing of components of a natural system. Description is typically used as a research method to explain unique natural systems (ecology or chemistry), large-scale phenomena (astronomy), or past events (geology).

Systematic Description

Systematic description is a component of almost every kind of scientific research. Description is helpful for questions when experimentation is impossible (e.g., determining events in earth history). Descriptive studies can be exploratory, in that hypothesis testing may not drive the research.

For example, recording daily observations of water levels in rivers or lakes is useful for addressing questions about events such as flood recurrence intervals or seasonal fluctuations.

When conducting an experiment, begin by describing the system/s that will be the focus of your investigation. Descriptions lead to information about the function or form of phenomena and the establishment of physical, spatial, and temporal relationships.

For digital studies, geographic research is ideally suited to methodological approaches that use geotagging, geocoding, and online maps.

History

Digital geographical technologies and online maps may also enhance historical studies. For example, your investigation of the history of the city

RESEARCH IN ACTION · Elizabeth's story

Elizabeth's undergraduate capstone project in geography grew out of her experience participating in a "citizen science" project. Citizen science is research that uses amateurs to gather scientific data.

For two years, Elizabeth had been a member of a network of volunteer amateur naturalists monitoring the condition of streams at sites throughout the Rouge River watershed in Toronto. Several days a month, she collected and recorded stream data for the database of the Ontario Ministry of Natural Resources (MNR). Using the Ontario Stream Assessment Protocol (OSAP; Stanfield 2010) created by the MNR, Elizabeth's group gathered and documented stream morphology (e.g., depth and velocity of water, features of the channel and bank, and vegetation and rate of plant growth), collected data about benthic macroinvertebrates or benthos (aquatic fauna such as insects, worms, and snails), carried out surveys of fish, and tracked water temperature.

The goal of the project was to build knowledge about ecosystems and issues such as stormwater and invasive aquatic species that degrade the watershed. Elizabeth's contribution to the project was to put on waders, step into a stream, check a net, and count and weigh benthos while noting cloud cover, precipitation, temperature of the air and water, and clarity and conditions of the stream.

Through this experience, she learned that the Jefferson salamander (*Ambystoma jeffersonianum*) was a nationally endangered species. She decided to focus her digital project on the "Jeffs," as she called the salamanders, and to take advantage of the MNR database.

Elizabeth began the Methodology section of her digital essay by stating her purpose:

> The purpose of this study is to analyze long-term data trends to better understand how urban encroachment on natural habitats impacts landscape form and stream ecology, placing species at risk of extinction.

She then explained and justified her focus on the salamanders:

The *Ambystoma jeffersonianum* is under threat across North America. In Canada, the salamanders are found only in Ontario.

She went on to defend her choice of the site for her research:

For this reason the Rouge River watershed provides a unique opportunity to investigate changes to the natural ecosystem that put pressure on rare species when urban boundaries extend into natural habitats.

The next statements in Elizabeth's Methodology section underscored the importance of this research and its significance for geography:

New insights can be applied to the development of landscape practices, designs, policies, and technologies that in future will improve our ability to protect natural environments, ecosystems, ecological processes, and at-risk species.

Having explained the purpose of her study, justified her site selection and choice of species, and highlighted the importance of the research, Elizabeth went on to explain how she would be using global positioning systems (**GPS**) and geographic information systems (**GIS**) to georeference the site location.

Geographical coordinates—latitude and longitude or the Universal Transverse Mercator (UTM)—will be gathered through the use of a global positioning system (GPS). Certain units offer only uncorrected coordinates, and it may require up to 15 minutes per site to identify locations. Correcting coordinates is necessary before data can be used in geographic information systems (GIS).

After writing several paragraphs describing how she would be using the technology to identify the site location, Elizabeth turned her

Continued . . .

attention to an explanation of why—relative to other, alternative tools—the OSAP was the optimal instrument for collection of data for her study:

> The Ontario Ministry of Natural Resources (MNR) created the Ontario Stream Assessment Protocol (OSAP; Stanfield 2010) in order to standardize and simplify data collection, methods of documentation, and analysis. While other protocols exist, no other tool is both freely available and connected to a standardized database that is open and accessible to the public and updated on a regular basis.

Next, Elizabeth described the data collection procedures, referencing the OSAP, and then concluded at the end of her Methodology section:

> The conditions that threaten the Jefferson salamander in the Rouge River watershed offer an unusual opportunity to gain insight into environmental protection, conservation, and restoration through research and monitoring. The overall objective of this study is to further environmental and ecological understanding; this will lead to improved decision making concerning vulnerable species and will ensure a sustainable future.

Jefferson salamander (*Ambystoma jeffersonianum*).

of London, England, could combine geographical and visual techniques to show how the city grew and changed over time.

Primary and Secondary Sources of Historical Information

Historians do not address questions of methodology in the same way as some other researchers who use qualitative or quantitative methods (Rousmaniere 2004). In historical disciplines, the main methodological concerns focus on sources, the various types of historical data that are or were available, and the ways in which data are interpreted.

There are two main groups of sources, primary and secondary. Primary sources are closest to the topic, generated at the time of the event or by the subject in question. Secondary sources are removed from the historical event in time and place and often interpret primary sources. The type of sources used and the way they are interpreted depends on the research objectives and the theory that guides the research.

Historiography

Historiography involves "the study of the techniques of historical research and historical writing" (Rousmaniere 2004, 33). In other words, historiography involves critical reflection on the "history of writing about history."

Interdisciplinary, Transdisciplinary, and Multidisciplinary Studies

In **interdisciplinary research**, the problem, question, or theme defines the approach adopted and directs efforts to find a synthesis across subject, field, or disciplinary divisions.

Interdisciplinary methods of research contrast with **transdisciplinary research**, where real life contexts—such as some actual problem or situation—guide investigations that extend beyond particular disciplinary boundaries.

Interdisciplinary research contrasts as well with **multidisciplinary research**, where disciplines are loosely linked by way of a problem, question, or theme, and there is little attempt to synthesize and integrate the diverse methods employed (Ontario Ministry of Education 2002, 4).

Linguistics

Ethnographic fieldwork is thought to be the only reliable method in the discipline of linguistics for collecting data about the way speech acts function in interactions between or among people. Ethnographic fieldwork (or observation) can be carried out using notes or via audio or video recordings.

Sociolinguistics

Sociolinguistics (the study of how society affects language) relies on a broad range of research techniques drawn from linguistics, sociology, dialectology, psychology, discourse analysis, stylistics, pragmatics, and language planning. Sociolinguistic studies also employ philosophical techniques and methods from psychology to conduct research from a positivist perspective.

Positivism

Positivism is a research paradigm that views information gained through the senses, logic, and mathematics as primary sources. Sense data that is verified is referred to as empirical evidence.

Positivism in sociolinguistics is the view that society and language are governed by general laws just as in the physical universe. Positivist methods typically involve gathering data using experimental techniques or surveys, and analyzing it using statistical methods.

Pragmatics

Pragmatics investigates the manner in which context contributes to meaning. Techniques include examining speech acts and functions using elicitation techniques such as role playing and completion tasks. If you use sociolinguistic methods, you will need to use experimental designs and statistical data analyses to identify the use of social rules observed by native and non-native speakers. Statistical techniques lend themselves to computationally intensive research.

Medicine

Statistical assessment of evidence is widely used in clinical medicine and epidemiology. A treatment for a disease can be compared to another treatment in a clinical trial and then compared again statistically. Due to ethical considerations and possible implications of consequences of treatments for participants, in many instances epidemiologists must work with non-experimental data, which may create difficulties in interpreting causal mechanisms of a condition.

In the fields of pharmacology and toxicology, scientific experiments are used to determine the relationship between a particular dosage and the body's response to it, known as the **dose-response relationship** of a new drug or chemical. Researchers perform experiments in which a population of organisms, such as laboratory mice, is separated into groups and each group is exposed to a different amount of a drug or chemical. Data that result from these experiments are compared to determine the degree of the organism's response to the dose of the substance administered.

Clinical Trials

Clinical trials are studies that follow selected individuals for a specific period of time. Some individuals receive an intervention while members of a control group do not. Most commonly used in medical, pharmaceutical, and public health research, clinical trials are often employed to measure the effects of medical interventions using therapeutic agents, devices, and procedures. A major part of the design of clinical trials involves the provision of mechanisms and procedures for maximizing and assessing compliance (how carefully someone adheres to a regimen of treatment or a course of medication).

New technologies can facilitate different phases of clinical research.

Nursing

Nursing uses qualitative methods to explore meanings, patterns, and relationships related to universal lived experiences as well as evidence-based approaches to medicine, health, and disease. Interviews and participant observation are also widely used to collect data. Content analysis (of interviews, surveys, and focus groups) is used for analyzing the multifaceted phenomena studied in nursing.

Philosophy

The discipline of philosophy involves the study of basic problems, such as the nature of reality, human existence, knowledge, morals, ethics, values, and language. Philosophy responds to basic problems by way of critical, systematic approaches that employ the principles of logic. Evidence is organized in ways that support a rational argument.

Deductive and Inductive Reasoning

Logical arguments use the principles of deductive or inductive reasoning. **Deductive reasoning** starts with a hypothesis or with known facts and proceeds to a conclusion from that generalization. The basic assumption in deductive reasoning is that if something is true of a class of things in general, this will apply to all the specific members of that class.

Inductive reasoning moves in the opposite direction, beginning with specific observations of one particular case and then moving toward broad generalizations.

Political Science

Political science is another methodologically diverse discipline. Research methods include fieldwork, survey research, statistical analysis, case studies, comparisons, interviews, content analysis, and model building. In all of these, traditional approaches can be adapted and translated to digital media.

Evaluation Research Methods

Policy research in political science frequently draws on evaluation research methods, which are used for assessing the effectiveness of social programs related to education, social welfare, health, housing, legal services, and economic development.

The purpose of evaluation research is to measure the effects of a program against the goals it set out to accomplish. Evaluation provides a means of contributing to subsequent decision-making so as to improve future programs. Evaluation compares what is with what should be. As the researcher, you try to remain unbiased in order to assess the phenomena that demonstrate whether the program under study did or did not achieve the intended goals. Thus, evaluation research is concerned with measuring results.

Psychology

Research methods in psychology include interviews, observational research, or case studies, which can be either **cross-sectional** (involving the study of all members of a population—or a representative subset—at one particular point in time), or **longitudinal** (involving repeated observations of the same things over long time periods).

Experimental research in psychology employs several types of measurements such as rate of response, reaction time, and other psychometric quantities. In cognitive psychology, the primary method is experimentation with human participants. Different kinds of thinking are studied under controlled conditions (e.g., the way in which people form and apply concepts or the performance of individuals attempting to solve puzzles).

Experimental research methods aim to determine how and why something happens or the way that an independent variable affects a dependent variable. Remember to use random samples representative of the population you are studying so as to avoid experimental bias.

Statistical surveys are also used to measure attitudes and traits, as well as changes in mood. Additionally, cognitive psychologists develop computational models that simulate aspects of human performance.

Sociology

The discipline of sociology is a social science that employs empirical, critical, analytical, and experimental research approaches, as well as quantitative and qualitative methods. Ethnographic approaches involve field research to depict the characteristics of a group or population as fully as possible.

Case Studies

In case study research, the focus is on an individual or small group of individuals with an unusual condition, in a unique situation, or alternatively, that can be seen as representative of many cases of the same type. Although in general, case studies are highly descriptive and thus qualitative, longitudinal research might involve repeated observations of the same variables over long periods of time. These observations are then interpreted using quantitative methods such as descriptive statistics.

Case studies are widely used in a number of fields, including social work, law, business and management, political science, and psychology. In many disciplines, a case study is an exemplary instance that has precedents or principles that can be applied to other, similar examples.

Cross-Sectional Research

The survey method is sometimes referred to as cross-sectional research. It can be employed when some phenomenon (the major independent variable) is observed, but the researcher does not have control over its variation. Data obtained from surveys is analyzed to identify similarities, differences, and trends and to make predictions about the group studied.

Surveys are carried out to obtain information from randomly selected respondents through group-administered pencil and paper questionnaires, face-to-face and telephone interviews, self-administered questionnaires online, or some other techniques of data collection to produce quantitative assessments. Descriptive and inferential statistics are used to evaluate research hypotheses.

Interviews

Interviews are similar to surveys but seek to obtain more in-depth information. Studies that involve in-depth interviews are viewed as using a qualitative approach. The participant provides information through verbal interchanges or conversations. Usually non-verbal behaviours and the interview context become part of the data equation. The most common interview type is the semi-structured interview: a general structure is established for the interview, but extra, spontaneous questions that emerge from the interaction with the interviewee can also be asked.

Interviews provide an opportunity to videotape the encounter (with permissions). Rather than presenting the entire interview as it took place, key sections are typically excerpted for the digital presentation. Typically, viewers will want to see the nuggets that are most relevant to your argument rather than the whole interview.

Interviews provide an opportunity to integrate motion pictures into your research and to experiment with digital editing software.

Observational Methods

Observational research methods have the researcher/s directly watching participants' reactions in a laboratory (laboratory observation, such as in psychology) or in a natural setting (naturalistic observation). Observational research increases the likelihood that participants will give honest accounts of the experiences or that they will take the study seriously. When selecting volunteer participants, take steps to make sure they are representative of the general public, or results will be biased.

Triangulation

A discussion of methods would not be complete without at least mentioning triangulation, which is used in some research studies to enhance the trustworthiness of the findings. Triangulation involves using multiple sources and perspectives to reduce the chance of bias.

There are four main types of triangulation:

- by source (data is collected from different sources);
- by methods (different data collection strategies are used such as individual interviews, focus groups, and participant observation);
- by researcher (more than one researcher analyzes the data or develops and tests the coding scheme); and
- by theories (multiple theories and perspectives are considered during data analysis and interpretation).

Triangulation serves to check errors and biases that skew results of a study.

The Big Picture: Creating the Total Project

After completing the Methodology section, you move beyond the components of the essay that you drafted for the project proposal and into new intellectual territory. Five or six major parts of the research essay come after the Methodology section. First is the Analysis or Body of the study, which is the analysis or examination portion of the investigation. Next is the Results or Findings section. Results are followed by the Conclusion. If you have formatted your document with endnotes, these references come after the Conclusion and before the Bibliography. If you have used footnotes, the Bibliography (or References section) is placed after the Conclusion. Appendixes are the final component of the digital essay. As you work to develop the entire project, your aim is to complete all the sections to a uniform standard and to forge connections among the various components to create a consistent and coherent product.

Components of the Essay that Follow the Methodology

The remaining components of the digital essay include the following:

- Analysis or Body of the study;
- Results or Findings;
- Conclusion;
- Endnotes (if applicable);
- Bibliography; and
- Appendix (if applicable).

To work effectively on the total document, visualize your project as a completed whole and as an interconnected fabric composed of component parts. Then, shift focus to concentrate on each of the component parts in turn, noticing the junctures where one component is connected to others.

Continually reassess what needs to be done relative to your vision of the big picture and work on developing the details in each of the component parts. As you gain skill and mastery of your topic, gradually bring each of the sections up to the same level of completeness, and polish them until the essay matches as closely as possible the product you envision.

Developing the Total Project

Superior projects meet four requirements. First, they are clearly focused on the topic with no major digressions; there is a unity of subject matter. Second, all the information the reader needs to know about your topic is set forth in the essay. In other words, the study is finished and it accomplishes what you set out to do. Third, the sections and paragraphs in the study follow an order that readers can recognize and understand. Finally, the paragraphs within a section are coherent; that is, they are arranged so readers can comprehend each section as a unit rather than as a collection of separate and disjointed paragraphs.

Unity

In an essay, unity entails thorough and consistent development of the concepts and ideas that the essay set out to explain. The essay in its entirety should focus on those concepts and ideas. In order to achieve this focus, each paragraph should show a clear connection to the main topic or governing ideas in the investigation and to the paragraphs that go before and come after.

Completeness

Completeness is a relative quality that can only be determined by considering the amount of information required to respond to the question. The goal is to provide sufficient information and details to fully explicate the topic but no more information than is needed to respond to the question.

Sequence

Sequence concerns the order of the sections and paragraphs in the essay. In a carefully constructed essay, the sections are ordered in a way that will make sense to the reader and the paragraphs move in a consistent direction so that the relationship among them is clear.

Whether perusing books or electronic documents and online formats, readers might not move through the pages or screens of the essay in a linear sequence. For example, a reader might read most of the Introduction, fast-forward to the Conclusion, look at the Bibliography, and then sample one or more sections in the middle of the piece. However, even in cases such as these, readers expect a certain sequencing of information whether or not they look at each section in the order they appear in your paper.

Coherence

Coherence, or *cohering,* means sticking together. Coherence refers to logical, orderly, aesthetically consistent relationships and interconnections among the parts. An essay is coherent when the sections and paragraphs move from one to the next so that readers have the impression of a synthetic whole, rather than a collection of unrelated pieces.

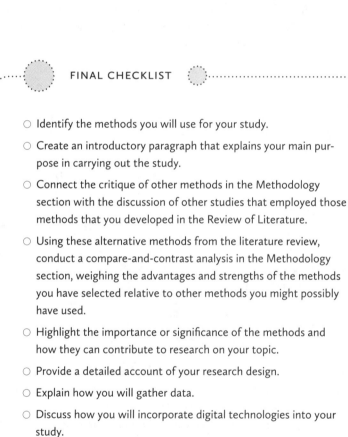

FINAL CHECKLIST

- ○ Identify the methods you will use for your study.
- ○ Create an introductory paragraph that explains your main purpose in carrying out the study.
- ○ Connect the critique of other methods in the Methodology section with the discussion of other studies that employed those methods that you developed in the Review of Literature.
- ○ Using these alternative methods from the literature review, conduct a compare-and-contrast analysis in the Methodology section, weighing the advantages and strengths of the methods you have selected relative to other methods you might possibly have used.
- ○ Highlight the importance or significance of the methods and how they can contribute to research on your topic.
- ○ Provide a detailed account of your research design.
- ○ Explain how you will gather data.
- ○ Discuss how you will incorporate digital technologies into your study.
- ○ Identify the problems or issues that might possibly skew the data.
- ○ End the Methodology section with a summary or with concluding remarks.

Chapter Summary

This chapter focused on the research methods specific to various disciplines. We explained how the discussion of methods you carried out in the Review of Literature is linked to the method/s you will employ in your study. We also explained that you will need to describe how you will incorporate new media and technologies into your scholarly work. Use of particular methods is defended and justified by explaining the advantages relative to other, competing methods. Working with the project as a whole, you began to integrate all the sections of your study into a project that is unified, coherent, ordered, and complete.

13

Analysis, Results, and Conclusion

Chapter Outline

Chapter Thirteen explains how to pull together the components of your project so that your vision is realized. The focus is on the major sections of the research essay that follow the Review of Literature and the Methodology sections. It is not possible to offer firm guidelines for these later sections of the digital essay, as they depend on the ways you are investigating your subject area. Every essay is an original analysis of a topic; each discipline has particular requirements for scholarly writing, and so the best works in your discipline provide the models for your original study. We do present some of the key features of the subsequent sections, offer suggestions about structuring them, and explain how to create links among the various sections of the investigation. Finally, we discuss completing and polishing the project and attaching relevant documents as appendixes. A checklist helps you assemble all the pieces in order to submit an outstanding and finished piece of work.

Creating a Coherent Study

The explanations, critique, and criteria developed in the Review of Literature and Methodology will provide the pivot upon which the later sections of your digital essay turn.

If any principle, concept, idea, issue, or criterion is a focus of discussion in the Analysis or Body of the study and was not mentioned in the Review of Literature, go back and revise the earlier sections of your essay so they anticipate and foreshadow your later analysis of these concepts. Similarly, if a concept appears in the Review of Literature but not in the Analysis or Body of the study, either add the concept to the Analysis or Body or remove it from the Review of Literature.

Creating Links among Parts of the Study

Constructing bridges between the information in various sections of the essay is what creates unity and coherence. Screenwriters speak of such a connection as "the knife in the drawer." If the hero will need a knife to extricate himself from a tight situation at the end of a movie, screenwriters are careful to include a scene early on that shows the knife in the drawer—or someone placing it there—so viewers are not surprised. If the implement suddenly and conveniently appears without forewarning at the end, the audience feels cheated at the clumsy plot device. When the camera lens zeroes in and pauses for a few seconds near the beginning of the movie on something that seems ordinary or a detail, this is "a knife in a drawer" that alerts viewers that it will be a major element or hinge in the plot at some point in the film.

Similarly, a film crew always includes a continuity person to check that visuals are consistent over multiple takes. If a soldier has a bandage on his left eye at the beginning of a scene and in the same scene it switches to his right eye—perhaps because different takes of that scene were shot over the course of several days—the audience is jarred out of the fictional world the film has created. These sorts of disruptions and discontinuities in your own study will mar your final product unless they are smoothed over and polished so the reader does not notice that different parts were created at different times.

Seek to build connections and continuities among the components of your study to create a finished and quality project.

Linking Different Sections

Just as you look back to the Introduction, Review of Literature, and Methodology sections and create connecting statements as you develop the Analysis or Body of the study, so you look ahead to the Results or Findings section of your project in order to include statements that dovetail with other parts of the study.

The meaning and import of the material in the Analysis or Body and the Results or Findings sections goes in the Conclusion. This culminating section of the study typically reworks the thesis statement presented in your Introduction so that it reflects the thinking that came out of your analysis and findings. The Bibliography is a formal list of all the sources you cited in the course of your study. The Appendix offers additional information that is relevant to the research in the essay.

The Analysis or Body of the Study

As an approximate guide, the Analysis or Body of the study ranges from 10 to 14 pages in a typical 7,000 word or 20 to 25-page essay or article. As you embark on this analysis component of the inquiry, think of it as another mini-essay. Like the Review of Literature and Methodology sections, it should have its own brief introduction and summary of results, even as it is vitally tied to other parts of the essay through transitions and connections.

Argument and Persuasion

Since a characteristic shared by many academic essays across a number of disciplines is the style of writing known as the argumentative or persuasive essay, the body of your research project will likely have as a major aim the presentation of data, facts, and other kinds of evidence, organized in a way that is designed to convince readers to accept your argument or point of view. The goal is to compel readers—through the force of persuasion—to come around to your position.

The Thesis Emerges from the Analysis of the Evidence

Different kinds of scholarly essays—such as cause and effect, comparison and contrast, definition and classification, and critical—were described in Chapter Eight. Again, use the evidence and findings in your study to determine the thesis, argument, and conclusions of your paper. The thesis can develop, change, and evolve as your essay progresses.

Re-enact Your Investigation for Readers

In contrast to a thesis that remains static throughout the document, we suggest that the Analysis or Body re-enact for the reader the manner in which the investigation unfolded for you as a scholar, exposing your own streams of thought as you are gradually led to your conclusions.

To use another analogy, you might think of a persuasive essay as a kind of scholarly detective story or mystery tale, wherein you share with readers your initial perplexity in the face of the problem and then show them how you gradually arrived at your conclusions.

Connections among the Analysis, Hypothesis, and Thesis

Think of the hypothesis that you set forth in the Introduction as a kind of "hypothetical thesis." It presents your tentative explanation, response, answer, or solution to the problem—usually in a way that forms the basis of experiments or tests that might confirm or falsify its viability. The Review of Literature then highlights and critiques the previous lines of thinking proposed by your intellectual predecessors about the problem.

Next, in the body of your study, you clarify, disambiguate, question, extend, substantiate, qualify, and critique both your own initial thesis and the work that has come before you. This is accomplished by marshalling evidence and organizing it to support your argument—an argument that has emerged from this evidence.

What is the research telling you? What does the evidence suggest? How does your evidence differ from the evidence other scholars obtained in previous studies? Viable theses are typically an outcome of a struggle with the material; they are a consequence of careful analysis and interpretation of the data and evidence.

As you revise and create multiple drafts, think about ways that the ideas developing through your analysis might help you to further delimit the thesis, as well as make it more cogent and rigorous.

The Superior Argument: Kuhn's Criteria

As you carry on a dialogue with scholars in your discipline—both past and present—remember that the best explanation is one that can account for more evidence than rival theories. The greater the explanatory power of your account and the evidence that supports it relative to the alternative explanations suggested by other researchers, the more likely it will be that you will persuade readers to accept your argument and adopt your point of view.

Recall also that the strength of any theory or interpretation depends on how well its central ideas mesh with all the available evidence. This includes (1) material that others consider crucial; (2) evidence that exists but which other researchers did not view as relevant or did not include in their analysis; and (3) how well your evidence explains oddities and inconsistencies that cannot be explained by other theories.

These criteria serve as measures for gauging how well a particular view (especially your own) stacks up against alternative positions offered by other writers.

Apply Kuhn's criteria, both to your own thesis, arguments, and evidence and to those presented by your sources. Ask questions: "So what?" "What does this mean for the set of issues that come together as the problem?" "Does this fit with the observations I am making in this analysis?" "How does this help me in my effort to respond to the problem?" "For how much of the evidence can it account?" "What does not mesh with this theory?"

Evidence that Does Not Fit

When you find evidence that does not tally with either your thesis or the theses presented by other authors, try to explain exactly how and why it does not fit and the meaning of the mismatch. Do not simply ignore evidence that does not mesh. What are the factors or features that elude explanation?

Pause as your study progresses to reformulate or add precision and rigour to your thesis. If you can show that your account includes more of the evidence than alternative explanations include, even if it cannot account for all of the evidence, then your reader will likely accept your point of view—and hence your thesis and conclusions.

Claim and Evidence

There are a number of studies that explain how to develop a clear and logically persuasive argument, and so we are only able to provide an abbreviated discussion here. ◉ Think of your thesis statement (and also the Conclusion) as the major claim of the essay (Toulmin 1969).

The claim is the statement that the reader or viewer is asked to accept as accurate or true. The thesis or claim is supported by evidence that is gathered through a close reading (an analysis or interpretation) of the text (or image, film, screen, etc.) or phenomenon (e.g., a weather pattern or behaviour of cells) (Murray and Gibson 2010).

There are different kinds of claims (factual/definitional, policy, value), just as there are different kinds of evidence (statistics, examples, testimony). The arrows in the following figure highlight the relationship between claim and evidence. Starting with the claim, it might be argued that a claim is true because of certain evidence. Conversely, starting with the evidence, one might argue that given the analysis or interpretation of certain evidence, the claim must be true.

The relationship between claim, evidence, and warrant.

Claims and Warrants

The warrant is a logical and rhetorical device that links the evidence to the claim or to what must be presumed if the evidence is to provide strong support for the claim (see figure above).

Assessing the warrant is what requires the most skill. The warrant is often implicit or hidden, and it is the concealed or unstated nature of warrants that provides a major opportunity for you to expose weaknesses in the work of others, or conversely, for your professor to uncover weak or unfounded warrants in your essay.

Rhetorical Forms

In Chapter Eight, we identified three ways to persuade readers: gain their trust, appeal to their emotions, or present valid reasons so they are convinced by the logic of your argument.

Aristotle referred to these three main rhetorical forms as: *ethos*, *pathos*, and *logos*. The *ethos* relates to the trust or respect the reader has for the credibility or the authority of the writer. The *pathos* refers to how the argument appeals to the emotions. The *logos* concerns the facts, reasons, or logic deployed to support the argument (which can be inductive or deductive).

A couple of examples will serve as illustration. Some people claim that "medical marijuana ought to be legalized because there is evidence that it is effective in treating pain." The warrant that must be drawn out of this argument is an implicit claim (with its own evidence and warrant) about the relation between the law, on the one hand, and substances that effectively reduce pain, on the other.

Thinking about alternative examples shows the weakness of the argument: "Heroin effectively reduces pain, so heroin ought to be legalized for medical use" or "Euthanasia effectively reduces pain, so the practice of terminating a human life to end suffering ought to be made legal."

Learning to map arguments in this way provides a powerful tool for helping you understand the weaknesses and strengths in both your own position and in the positions presented by others.

The Results or Findings of the Study

Following the Analysis or Body of the study, the next major section is the Results or Findings. In a typical 20- to 25-page digital essay or article, the Results or Findings section should take up 1 to a maximum of 5 pages. In a thesis or dissertation, the Results or Findings section is a major chapter in the study. The paragraphs that set forth the results of your investigation will be the product of the analysis undertaken in the Analysis or Body of your study—and therefore unique to your particular project. Still, we can offer a few notes about how you might organize the presentation of your findings.

Response to the Question

Effectively written Results or Findings sections often present a response to the main elements of the Introduction: What is your answer to the research question? What is your solution to the problem you identified in the Introduction? Now that you have studied the issues thoroughly, how has the problem become either simpler or more complex?

If you were not able to resolve all of the issues that you pinpointed up front as being parts of the problem, why not? What would be required in order for you to offer an effective resolution? How does the analysis presented in the Analysis or Body section of your study relate to the thesis? How did the thesis evolve over the course of your investigation? If the thesis changed, in what ways did your formulation of it become more precise and rigorous and why? Did the original hypothesis turn out to be accurate or inaccurate, correct or incorrect?

Was the hypothesis confirmed or falsified? ◉ That is, did your analysis show that the hypothesis was correct, thereby confirming it? Or did the analysis demonstrate that the hypothesis was not correct, thereby falsifying it? You offered a statement of significance in the Introduction; how has your understanding of this significance been deepened, broadened, or enriched by the research you have undertaken? Why are your findings important? Who will be affected by your results? What is the potential impact of your research? Were the aims, goals, or purposes fulfilled or not?

Response to Limitations and Scope

If there are limitations to your research, you might want to restate them here. What were the assumptions (in the literature, in your own thinking)? Did these assumptions prove to be accurate or inaccurate, biased or objective? What about the methodology? Do you have suggestions for improvements that would overcome limitations?

The Conclusion of the Digital Essay

The last part of your study summarizes the main points made in your digital essay and then offers suggestions for further research.

Some concluding sections begin by summarizing and outlining the entire course of the investigation. Some begin with a forceful reformulation of the thesis statement and conclusions. Others might explain why the conclusion offers a more compelling account of the evidence. Almost all excellent concluding sections offer suggestions for further research.

In the final paragraphs of your paper, you may want to revisit the issues you mentioned in the very first paragraphs of the Introduction, explaining how they have been explained or resolved. What is the next step in the research? Explain to other investigators the avenues that your research has opened. And you may want to try to make sure the sentences at the end of your study provide the reader with a sense of completion.

Endnotes

The references are a significant component of the study. There are three basic formats for documenting citations in an academic paper:

- parenthetical citations;
- footnotes; or
- endnotes.

Again, exact formatting will depend on the style guide used by your discipline such as those published by the Modern Languages Association (the *MLA Handbook*), the University of Chicago (*The Chicago Manual of Style*), and the American Psychological Association ("APA Style"). Parenthetical citations are positioned inside the text, footnotes are numbered consecutively and appear at the bottom of each page, and endnotes are numbered as well and appear after the Conclusion but before the Bibliography.

Word processing software has greatly facilitated footnoting; pages are reformatted automatically with each change of the text. Creating hyperlinks to the referenced text is easy using both parenthetical citations and footnotes.

The Final Bibliography

Creating a bibliography is a complex and time-consuming endeavour, as you have likely discovered. Again, if you have been working with one of the digital citation managers such as RefWorks, EndNote, Zotero, or Mendeley, you will need to double-check every entry to correct errors in capitalization or formatting that inevitably result from automatic methods.

Working Bibliography versus Final Bibliography

Keep up with the process of generating and correcting entries all through the research process so that by the time you are ready to submit your final project, you have a comprehensive and accurate working bibliography.

The working bibliography includes all sources that you considered over the course of creating your project.

The final bibliography is the list, placed at the end (or if you have an appendix, in the penultimate position) of your study. The working bibliography is tentative and probably includes items that had little value for your investigation, items that were relevant but you did not actually cite in your study, and items that you referenced one or more times.

The final bibliography, by contrast, should only include the works you reference in the parenthetical citations (or endnotes or footnotes) of your document.

Your Digital Scholarly Archive

Why take the time to list and correct all the studies that you consult? First, if you have kept up with the formatting all along, you will be able to create a final bibliography, either by generating it automatically using computer-mediated methods or by quickly deleting those studies that you did not cite.

Second, when the deadline for your assignment is close and you are running out of time, you do not want to be fiddling with capitalization or worrying about the format for oddball entries that were garbled in

RefWorks and do not seem to conform to any of the rules in your style guide.

Third, if you continue to pursue research on this topic in the future, your working bibliography will prove invaluable. The topics that intrigued you for this digital project will likely continue to hold interest for you in the future. Listing and annotating even those studies that were of poor quality or unusable can save you time down the road. A simple annotation indicating the low quality of the information in that publication will prevent you from taking time to track down a book in the library only to find that you have once again spent time finding a work that intrigued with a promising title but turns out to have little value.

Think of this project as the first step in creating an archive that will serve you well as you continue with your scholarly career.

Appendix or Appendixes

At the very end of your document and following the Bibliography, or in a separate file in an electronic presentation, place any items that are crucial to your study or useful to the reader.

If your research involved human subjects, place the permissions and signed forms in an appendix.

Did you conduct a survey? Did you briefly mention the architectural features of a building that would be helpful to see in a photograph? Does it help the reader to have technical information about planning a research expedition to Antarctica? If you quote from interviews with Creole folk from the Sea Islands of South Carolina and northern Georgia, is it useful to have a glossary of expressions from the Gullah language? This material that is additional or supplementary to the information discussed in your essay should be placed at the back of the study (if on paper) or included as a distinct section (in a digital project).

Style and Substance

When you have a solid draft of the document with all of the components in place, it is time to concentrate on improving the **style** of your project. Style refers to the way something is said as opposed to the **substance**, which is the content and message of any communication. Style, in contrast to substance, is a matter of form rather than content—though it can be difficult to separate the two.

Readers often look at a number of articles on the same topic and then concentrate their attention on one or two essays that have intellectual substance and an aesthetic style. If the professor reads your essay as one of a number of studies received from class members, all of whom compete with you for good grades, writing style can be a major factor distinguishing your research from the competition.

Aim to balance readable style and substantive research while adhering to the generic conventions of your discipline. A paper that is beautifully written but lacking in substance misses the mark as surely as one that is well researched but contains vague sentences, awkward phrasings, and grammatical errors. Producing a thoroughly researched and carefully argued study with polished writing and stylistic flair will move your paper to the top of the grade scale for your class.

Revising and Polishing the Total Project

As the project comes together and you move from writing to editing and polishing your draft, bear in mind the four primary goals of academic writing: originality, clarity, consistency, and rigour.

Originality

Your work can be original even if your topic is mostly well-travelled intellectual territory. Using new digital technologies can help you bring fresh perspectives to topics through images, sounds, and links, even when the topics have received considerable scholarly attention in the past. You should be able to come up with some original ideas or a new slant that presents the matters under discussion in a new light by continually asking yourself questions: "How can I use new media to add details and interest?" "What are the techniques that would contribute to the creation of some fresh angle on my topic?" "What can I contribute that is new?" "What is my own take on these issues?" "What have others left out of the picture that I can add?" If you have seen an idea repeated over and over by different sources during the course of your research, try not to include that same idea stated in a similar way in your study.

For example, many studies of literature concentrate on the same passages in a text, which scholars have deemed crucial to understanding the work. To contribute something fresh, try focusing your analysis on the passages that come right before or just after those sections of the text. Or focus the lens at a wide angle and take in the passages that come before and after a key section of text as well as the ones that everyone else examines. Viewing crucial passages through a wider-angle lens can provide opportunities for insights that other scholars have missed.

Clarity

Look out for poor mechanics. Take advantage of the features built into your word processing software. Pay attention to green underlines (grammatical errors or cumbersome statements) or red underlines (spelling errors)—and use grammar and spelling checkers to fix awkward or vague sentence constructions or to correct outright mistakes.

Try reading your essay out loud. If you find yourself pausing and then rereading a sentence or going back over a paragraph to understand the meaning, rewrite that part of your study so that it flows smoothly and makes better sense on first reading.

To avoid contradictions in your writing, concentrate on the entire study and make sure that something you state earlier is not at odds with something you state later, and vice versa. Rereading your project from beginning to end will help you avoid the irregularities that can derail your argument and, indeed, your entire case.

Consistency

As the due date for your assignment draws near, concentrate on completing and polishing the essay components and on gradually building the transitions that fuse them together into a coherent and consistent whole.

To achieve consistency, all the sections of your project need to be written to the same level and standard. It may be helpful to separate your essay components into different files on your computer and to count the number of drafts you have put each section through by saving the file with a draft number—for example, "Conclusion Draft 9 Research Project. docx." That way, you will be able to stay on top of the sections that require more work so that the level of detail and quality is on par with all the other parts of the essay.

Students often do not realize that excellent essays have typically gone through dozens of drafts. This is not an exaggeration. In addition, know that about half of the time spent on an academic essay goes toward completing all of the details and polishing the writing—after the bulk of the essay has been completed.

This is why we underscore that writing is a recursive process and recommend that you do detailed work as you go along rather than leaving it for the end when you are pressed for time. Going over the digital essay many times and taking care of time-consuming details as you generate your study also lets you see the piece as a finished whole and to identify and remove lumps and bumps that prevent the project from gelling as a unity.

Rigour

By scholarly rigour, we are referring to the standards that professors expect for students and also the standards that you set for yourself in order to achieve the grades you are capable of earning. Concentrate on removing extra words and on making sure every word that you use is the one that is most appropriate to convey the ideas you want to communicate. You will find that with each draft, your writing becomes more accurate. As you reduce the number of words you use to express a concept, the writing will become more compressed.

Sharpness and Density

By sharp, we mean that the words you choose become progressively more precise relative to the meaning you envision in your mind's eye. By dense, we mean that the writing tightens to communicate complex ideas in fewer words, sentences, and paragraphs. Excellent scholarly writing is accurate, compressed, and lucid—it flows so that the reader's eye moves easily from one sentence and paragraph to the next—even if complex ideas are being communicated.

Check the Meaning of Every Word

Use a dictionary and a thesaurus to look up the meanings associated with every word that you use in your study. Inaccurate word usage is a sure sign of carelessness in scholarly writing.

Remove Jargon

Concentrate on minimizing the use of technical terms and jargon. Though you want to be well versed in the key terms in your field, nothing clouds a communication more than loading up your text with complex technical terms.

For the most part, good scholarly writing uses words to achieve exactitude and simplicity. Work that achieves originality, clarity, consistency, and rigour can be recognized as excellent by reading just a few paragraphs.

Finishing the Digital Essay

If you make sure that all of the sections of your digital essay are completed and that the writing exceeds expectations—for your discipline, your instructor, and yourself—you should be well positioned to earn a good grade. If you post your work on the Internet, your efforts to achieve a quality project will be rewarded by many hits and references to your work by other scholars.

RESEARCH IN ACTION · Carter's story

Carter's assignment in his third-year English course involved examining how Victorian novels reflected prevailing social and cultural attitudes and values. He decided to focus his argument on how Charles Dickens's serialized novels raised public awareness of previously unexamined social conditions in Victorian England.

As Carter's research got underway, he felt discouraged by the sheer volume of studies in Victorian fiction. Since so many other authors had concentrated on how Dickens had exposed the appalling working conditions created by the Industrial Revolution, Carter turned his attention to life in the country during this same time period. He decided to focus on the novel *The Old Curiosity Shop* and to contextualize his critical argument about the social role of entertainments in rural communities by using digital techniques.

Carter focused the lens of his inquiry on Nell's travels with the Punch and Judy show in Dickens's story. He combined his reading of the novel with other research on Dickens, travelling shows, and social economic history. The argument in Carter's essay developed a close and careful reading of sections of Dickens's text, and it referenced other texts, images, and documents focusing on attitudes and perceptions of actors and other performers as well as the ways that travelling carnivals and festivals contributed to social life during the Victorian period.

Carter used online maps to track the route taken by Nell as she travelled with the show, and he supplemented this material with a number of images, including drawings, etchings, and even early photographs of Victorian audiences observing performances. His digital essay provided links to these maps and images as well as a sound track of a Punch and Judy show that he located.

Carter developed a website for his project using the standard iWeb software that came with his Apple computer, and he also submitted a hard copy of his essay to his professor with the maps and images included as appendixes.

FINAL CHECKLIST

- ○ Complete all the parts of your study, bringing all the components up to the same standard, and creating links among the sections.
- ○ Finalize the title and subtitle.
- ○ Create a title page or screen.
- ○ Finalize the abstract.
- ○ Generate a table of contents with page numbers and links (if relevant).
- ○ Put the Introduction through a final polishing.
- ○ Double-check all references to ensure proper formatting and that the spelling of authors' names, the dates, and the page numbers of texts are correct.
- ○ Make sure there is a related bibliographic entry for each work cited in the references.
- ○ Edit the Review of Literature so that it includes only those arguments and discussions that are relevant to the analysis in the Analysis or Body of your study.
- ○ Review the Methodology section one more time to make sure that it resonates with the methods you employed to obtain your results.
- ○ The Analysis or Body of the study is the opportunity for you to "perform" your research, writing, and creative skills. Make sure your interpretation ties in with material in other sections of the study.
- ○ Formulate the Results or Findings section, bearing in mind the goals you set for yourself in the Introduction.
- ○ Create statements in every section that link to other parts of the study.
- ○ Create a powerful Conclusion. Try to make sure that the reader is rewarded for having continued reading your study all the way through to the end.
- ○ Make sure that the Bibliography is flawless.

Continued ...

- ○ Attach any supplementary documents or images that may be slightly tangential to the material in the main document as appendixes.
- ○ Triple-check to make sure that your name (and student number) or appropriate contact information are clearly visible in your study.
- ○ Flip through the entire assignment, making sure screens are formatted the way you intended or that there are no glitches on your paper document. See the document as a unity.
- ○ Congratulations! You are ready to hit the Send button, click on Submit, or walk a hard copy to the university.

Chapter Summary

This final chapter outlined the key sections of the research essay that follow the Introduction, Review of Literature, and Methodology sections. These are the Analysis or Body of the study, the Results or Findings, the Conclusion, the Endnotes (if relevant), the Bibliography, and the Appendix/es (if relevant). Describing how to bring together all the elements of the digital project, we explained how to work with the entire project in mind and construct effective connections between the different parts of the study so that it becomes a cohesive unity. We offered some tips about organizing the Analysis or Body of the essay and explained how this part of the investigation informs the Results or Findings section. We also explained why the Conclusion typically reformulates the thesis statement you initially presented in the Introduction so that it reflects the deeper understanding you acquired through the research and writing process. With our suggestions about finishing the final document and attaching appropriate appendixes, we have guided your research project to completion, and it is ready for submission.

References

Boyd, Danah M., and Nicole B. Ellison. 2007. "Social Network Sites: Definition, History, and Scholarship." *Journal of Computer-Mediated Communication* 13: 210–30. Retrieved 25 October 2011. http://jcmc.indiana.edu/vol13/issue1/boyd.ellison.html.

Comeforo, Kristin. 2010. "Review Essay: Manufacturing Consent: The Political Economy of the Mass Media." *Global Media and Communication* 6 (2): 218–230.

Doyle, Bob. 2006. "When to Wiki, When to Blog." *EContent* (July). Retrieved 24 October 2011. www.econtentmag.com/Articles/ArticlePrint.aspx?Article ID=16900.

Fountain, Renee. 2005. "Wiki Pedagogy." *Dossiers technopédagogiques*. Retrieved 24 October 2011. http://profetic.org/dossiers/article.php3?id_article=969.

Franklin, Tom, and Mark van Harmelen. 2007. "Web 2.0 for Content for Learning and Teaching in Higher Education." *JISC*. Retrieved 23 October 2011. http://repository.jisc.ac.uk/148/1/web2-content-learning-and-teaching.pdf.

Gephart, Robert. 1999. "Paradigms and Research Methods." *Research Methods Forum* 4. Academy of Management, Research Methods Division. http://division.aomonline.org/rm/1999_RMD_Forum_Paradigms_and_Research_Methods.htm.

Gibson, Twyla. 2009. "On Translation and Transformation: Media, Education, and the Continuity of Cultures." In *What's Next? Il lavoro dell'insegnante e le sue scelte nell'età dell'elettronica* [The Future of the University in the Electronic Age], edited by Francesco Guardiani. Ottawa: Legas Publishing.

Gold, Matthew K., ed. 2012. *Debates in the Digital Humanities*. Minneapolis, MN: University of Minnesota Press. http://dhdebates.gc.cuny.edu/debates.

Heisenberg, Werner. (1962) 2000. *Physics and Philosophy: The Revolution in Modern Science*. London: Penguin Books Ltd.

Hensley, Merinda K. 2011. "Citation Management Software: Features and Futures." *Reference & User Services Quarterly* 50 (3): 204–08. Retrieved 27 October 2011. http://rusa.metapress.com/content/k7tv4m7660n4438n/ fulltext.pdf.

Herman, Edward S., and Noam Chomsky. (1988) 2002. *Manufacturing Consent: The Political Economy of the Mass Media*, rev. ed. New York: Pantheon Books.

Kuhn, Thomas S. (1962) 1970. *The Structure of Scientific Revolutions*, 2nd ed. Chicago: University of Chicago Press.

Lamb, Brian. 2004. "Wide Open Spaces: Wikis, Ready or Not." *EDUCAUSE Review Online* 39 (5): 36–48. Retrieved 24 October 2011. www.educause.edu/ ero/article/wide-open-spaces-wikis-ready-or-not.

Lin, Yu-Wei. 2012. "Transdisciplinarity and Digital Humanities: Lessons Learned from Developing Text-Mining Tools for Textual Analysis." In *Understanding Digital Humanities*, edited by David M. Berry, 295–314. Houndmills, Basingstoke, UK: Palgrave Macmillan. http://usir.salford .ac.uk/19304/.

Lipton, Mark. 2013. "Doing Media Studies." In *Mediascapes: New Patterns in Canadian Communication*, 4th ed., edited by Leslie Regan Shade, 25–42. Toronto: Nelson.

McKiernan, Gerry. 2004. "Rich Site Services: Web Feeds for Extended Information and Library Services." *LLRX.com* (20 September). Retrieved 24 October 2011. www.llrx.com/features/richsite.htm.

Mitchell, Gail J. 1994. "Discipline-Specific Inquiry: The Hermeneutics of Theory-Guided Nursing Research." *Nursing Outlook* 42 (5): 224–28.

Murray, Stuart J., and Twyla Gibson. 2010. "Unknown Knowers: Mediating Knowledge in the 'Global Village.'" In *Epistemologies of Ignorance and Studies of Limits in Education*, edited by E. Malewski and N. Jaramillo, 199–220. Information Age Press.

Murthy, Dhiraj. 2008. "Digital Ethnography: An Examination of the Use of New Technologies for Social Research." *Sociology* 42 (5): 837–55.

Mylonas, Elli, Gregory Crane, Kenneth Morrell, and D. Neel Smith. 1993. "The Perseus Project: Data in the Electronic Age." In *Accessing Antiquity: The Computerization of Classical Studies*, edited by Jon Soloman. Tucson and London: The University of Arizona Press.

Naish, Richard. 2006. "Can Wikis Be Useful for Learning?" *e.learningage magazine* (May). www.qiconcepts.co.uk/wp-content/uploads/2010/07/ e-learning-2.0-using-new-internet-technogies-in-e-learning.pdf.

Nentwich, Michael. 2010. "Web 2.0 and Academia." In *Proceedings of the 9th Annual IAS-STS Conference: Critical Issues in Science and Technology Studies*. Graz, Austria, 3–4 May. http://epub.oeaw.ac.at/ita/ita-papers/ MN_10_1.pdf.

O'Loughlin, Rebecca. 2008. "The Relationship between Pedagogical and Discipline-Specific Research Methods: Critical Perspectives." *Discourse: Learning and Teaching in Philosophical and Religious Studies* 7 (2): 67–120.

Ontario Ministry of Education. 2002. *The Ontario Curriculum Grades 11 and 12: Interdisciplinary Studies*. www.edu.gov.on.ca/eng/curriculum/secondary/interdisciplinary1112curr.pdf.

Parker, Kevin R., and Joseph T. Chao. 2007. "Wiki as a Teaching Tool." *Interdisciplinary Journal of Knowledge and Learning Objects* 3: 57–72.

Rousmaniere, Kate. 2004. "Historical Research." In *Foundations for Research: Methods of Inquiry in Education and the Social Sciences*, edited by Kathleen deMarrais and Stephen D. Japan, 31–51. London: Lawrence Erlbaum.

Schwartz, Linda, Sharon Clark, Mary Cossarin, and Jim Rudolph. 2004. "Educational Wikis: Features and Selection Criteria." *International Review of Research in Open and Distance Learning* 5 (1): n.p.

Stanfield, Les, ed. 2010. *Ontario Stream Assessment Protocol, Version 8.0*. Peterborough, Ontario: Ontario Ministry of Natural Resources, Fisheries Policy Section. www.mnr.gov.on.ca/stdprodconsume/groups/lr/@mnr/@letsfish/documents/document/226871.pdf.

Technorati. 2011. "State of the Blogosphere 2011." *Technorati Media*. Retrieved 9 August 2012. http://technorati.com/social-media/article/state-of-the-blogosphere-2011-part1/.

Toulmin, Stephen. 1969. *The Uses of Argument*. Cambridge, England: Cambridge University Press.

Tschofen, Monique. 2008. "'Agents of Aggressive Order': Letters, Hands, and the Grasping Power of Teeth in the Early Canadian Torture Narrative." *MediaTropes* 1 (1): 19–41. www.mediatropes.com/index.php/Mediatropes/issue/view/174.

Vander Wal, Thomas. 2004. "Folksonomy Coinage and Definition." *Vanderwal. net* (2 February). Retrieved 23 October 2011. http://vanderwal.net/folksonomy.html.

Voss, Jakob. 2007. "Tagging, Folksonomy and Co—Renaissance of Manual Indexing?" Paper submitted to the *10th International Symposium for Information Science*, Cologne, Germany, 30 May–1 June.

Weinberger, David. 2005. "Tagging and Why It Matters." *Berkman Center for Internet and Society*. Retrieved 24 October 2011. http://cyber.law.harvard.edu/home/2005-07.

Williford, Christa, and Charles Henry. 2012. *One Culture: Computationally Intensive Research in the Humanities and Social Sciences*. Washington, DC: Council on Library and Information Resources. www.clir.org/pubs/reports/pub151.

Winer, David. 2002. "What Is a News Aggregator?" *DaveNet* (8 October). http://scripting.com/davenet/2002/10/08/whatIsANewsAggregator.html.

Woolf, Bobby. 2006. "Blog or Wiki?" *IBM developerWorks* (13 June). www.

ibm.com/developerworks/community/blogs/marybeth/entry/blog_or_
wiki?lang=en.

Young, Pat. 2010. "Generic or Discipline-Specific? An Exploration of the
Significance of Discipline-Specific Issues in Researching and Developing
Teaching and Learning in Higher Education." *Innovations in Education and
Teaching International* 47 (1): 115–24.

Glossary

abstract a brief summary of a research article or other scholarly communication, typically a 250 to 500 word outline at the beginning of an essay that summarizes the key aspects of the entire paper. Abstracts also serve as a form of proposal for academic conferences, collected anthologies, or special issues that focus on a theme or a problem.

academic integrity the moral code and ethical policy of academia, or the honesty, truthfulness, accuracy, and ethical standards you observe when pursuing your research.

addenda separate sheets of paper inserted into a print document that indicate corrections in the text.

aggregators websites or software that collect and analyze information from multiple sources.

analysis a process of separating a text into its component parts so as to engage in a detailed examination of those parts for the purposes of discussion and interpretation.

API (application programming interface) specifies how software components should communicate with each other.

application-conditioned delivery specific methods by which "apps" or applications are distributed.

argument taking a side in a debate or making a case and then defending your stand using persuasive evidence.

bitmap a digital image in a rectangular array of pixels.

blog   a website where individuals or groups post opinions and information on an ongoing basis.

blogosphere   the interlinking of blogs, bloggers, and readers posting comments.

blogrolls   links to other blogs that the blog owner reads or follows.

born-digital   material that originates in a digital form. This is in contrast to analogue (or print) material that has been digitized.

brick-and-mortar models of research   research that requires in-person visits to a building to access and view material.

call numbers   the numbers used by libraries for the classification of materials (e.g., the Dewey Decimal or Library of Congress Classification systems).

clinical trials   studies that follow selected participants for a specific period of time; some participants receive an intervention and some do not (the control group). Clinical trials measure the effects of medical interventions, including therapeutic agents, devices, and procedures.

cloud computing   software stored and delivered through a remote network.

CMS (content management system)   a web content publishing and management system that allows content originators to create, submit, and publish their content directly within a web application or site without any development tools or knowledge of HTML.

computer archives   a collection of individual publications often catalogued and made accessible in some way.

content analysis   a technique for gathering and analyzing the content of speeches, texts, images, and other media. The content can be words, sentences, paragraphs, pictures, or arguments, and the content analysis can be either qualitative or quantitative. See also QUALITATIVE CONTENT ANALYSIS and QUANTITATIVE CONTENT ANALYSIS.

Creative Commons   a licence that makes information available without charge to everyone with a computer.

critical   descended from a Greek word meaning to choose, separate, or discern. A critical essay is a piece of writing that seeks to investigate, analyze, interpret, and evaluate a topic.

cross-sectional research   research that involves the study of all members of a population, or a representative subset, at one particular point in time.

database aggregators   gather together (i.e., aggregate) research articles from many different sources and journals. You can search multiple databases at the same time or work with a single database depending on your discipline or your area of inquiry.

databases   structured sets of data or information contained in a computer system or online.

deductive reasoning   reasoning that starts with a hypothesis or known facts and proceeds to a conclusion from that generalization. The basic assumption in deductive reasoning is that if something is true of a class of things in general, this will apply to all the specific members of that class.

digital essay   the term we use when talking about scholarship that incorporates creative digital techniques and tools in an integrative framework.

digital ethnography   the application of new technologies to the method of ethnography. More specifically, digital ethnography describes the process and methodology of doing ethnographic research in a digital space.

discourse communities   scholarly groups that draw on particular information, texts, and techniques as background to the study of certain phenomena.

dose-response relationship   in the fields of pharmacology and toxicology, scientific experiments that are used to determine the relationship between a particular dosage and the body's response to it.

eBooks   electronic versions of printed books.

eJournals   electronic issues of journals and articles, either web versions of print documents or so-called born-digital publications.

empirical investigation   research that involves gaining knowledge by direct or indirect observation or experience.

essay   derived from the French word *essayer*, which means to try or to attempt. It stems from the Latin *exigere*—to drive out, to try, or to examine. In the English language, the term *essay* first meant a trial or an attempt.

ethnography   an established method of participant observation based on field research and has as its aim a full depiction of the characteristics of a group or population. Ethnographic research involves the process of describing a population's culture or way of life as a distinct point of view.

exposition   a form of writing that elucidates a topic by providing a thorough description that avoids bias, opinion, critique, or argument.

folksonomy   a collection of tags built up by users tagging information.

genre   the rules and conventions that situate modes of inquiry within various disciplinary paradigms. These different styles and forms for communicating information have evolved over time to represent knowledge efficiently and effectively to readers and audiences in a specific field.

geocoding   taking a geographic identifier, such as a street address or postal code, and finding associated geographic coordinates (or vice versa for reverse geocoding).

geotagging   the adding of geographical identification metadata to various types of digital media such as photos, videos, podcasts, websites, SMS messages, blog entries, or social network posts. The data typically consists of latitude and longitude coordinates, but it can also include altitude, accuracy data, and place names.

GIS (geographic information system)   designed to capture, store, manipulate, analyze, manage, and present all types of geographical data.

GPS (global positioning system)   positioning technologies made possible by satellites orbiting the earth that transmit information about geographic location and time.

hashtags   the hashtag symbol, #, marks keywords or tags, particularly those associated with microblogging sites such as Twitter.

hearsay   information gathered without the evidence—citations, references, or fact-checking—that proves its truth or validity.

HTML (HyperText Markup Language)   a system that allows pages to be displayed in a web browser. HTML is used to tag text and images in angle brackets <html> so that a web browser can read the document and organize it into a web page. The HTML tags are invisible from the web page; the browser does not display them but rather, uses HTML tags to interpret the content of the page.

hyperlinked documents   documents that allow readers to delve more deeply into the research and to directly access the images and other sources of information used in creating the body of evidence for a document or study.

inductive reasoning   a line of thought that begins with specific observations of one particular case and then moves toward broad generalizations.

infographics   graphics that present complex information and data sets in a visually stimulating and easy-to-digest design.

interdisciplinary research   research in which the problem, question, or theme defines the approach adopted and directs efforts to find a synthesis across subject, field, or disciplinary divisions.

LAN systems   (local area network) a network that links computers in a smaller area, such as a university.

LBS (location-based services)   services that integrate geographic location with the user's own context (e.g., city, town, college campus) to deliver precise information about buildings, restaurants, health services, or recreational opportunities at a certain place in real time.

longitudinal research   research that involves repeated observations of the same phenomena over long time periods.

metacognition   the term for higher order thinking. It is "thinking about thinking."

metadata   information about the data (e.g., publishing dates, authorship, purpose, or location) on a network.

method   a procedure, instrument, technique, tool, or manner of data collection used to study facts or evidence.

methodology   the describing, explaining, assessing, or critiquing of the standard processes, concepts, theories, or methods associated with a discipline. Moreover, a methodology involves examining or questioning the reasons or assumptions that form the intellectual underpinning of a specific theory or method.

mobile technologies   technology used for cellular communication.

models   scholarly materials that supply a plan, paradigm, pattern, or blueprint for mapping, organizing, and constructing your own original study.

multicasting   sending the same file to multiple users at the same time.

multidisciplinary research   research in which disciplines are loosely linked by way of a problem, question, or theme and there is little attempt to synthesize and integrate the diverse methods employed.

multimodal   a multimodal document or interface provides multiple media or tools for the communication of information (e.g., a message that incorporates still and moving images, music, sound effects, voices, and written text).

news aggregator   a website or software that collects and analyzes news from many different online sources and finds what is new.

OCR (optical character recognition)   the mechanical or electronic conversion of scanned images of handwritten, typewritten, or printed text into machine-encoded text. It is widely used as a form of data entry from original paper data sources, such as documents or printed records.

ontologies   a framework for knowledge representation wherein systems of classifications are arranged in hierarchies that move from general to specific.

open-source   software that uses source code that allow documents to be accessible to everyone free of charge over the internet.

OPML (Outline Processor Markup Language)   an XML format for outlines that makes it possible to share feed lists or a subject-specific feeds list with others.

paradigm   the idea that a theory, method, or even a specific case serves as a model for examining other like things that appear to be of the same type (i.e., "setting them side by side"). From the Greek word *paradeigma*, which means pattern, exemplar, or to exhibit by setting side by side.

participant observation   a research method that involves the direct observation of individuals or groups of people in their natural settings.

persuasive argument   a common format for scholarly writing across all the disciplines. Academic essays typically seek to shape communication in ways that help bring about a voluntary change in the reader's judgment. The aim is to turn the readers' thinking around so they accept a position they did not hold before.

pixels   short for "picture elements," the smallest individual unit in an image. Each pixel represents the colour (in colour images) or grey level (for black and white images) at a single point in the picture.

podcast   a series of audio or video media files (such radio programs or segments, lectures, news, or music) that are released episodically and typically downloaded by web syndication. A podcast is also a digital media file, either audio or video, that is freely available for download from the Internet.

qualitative content analysis   a method used to explore the meanings of messages. Data samples usually consist of purposively selected texts, which inform the research questions under investigation. Whereas QUANTITATIVE methods use computational approaches, qualitative studies seek to identify the specific themes that illustrate the range of the meanings of phenomena under investigation.

quantitative content analysis   a method of research that relies on counting manifest textual elements. For example, content analyses may track the number of times specific words are mentioned or the regularity of the appearance of particular concepts. Images may be analyzed as "visual texts." See also QUALITATIVE CONTENT ANALYSIS.

raster image or **raster map**   a two-dimensional array of small integers. These values are often transmitted or stored in a compressed form.

remote backup services   a way to store and share folders containing a number of documents for collaborative work.

research strategy   multiple tactics for information-seeking and for developing critical skills. Information-seeking entails understanding what information you need, where to look for it, and how to use it effectively to solve problems.

RSS feeds   an initialism for Really Simple Syndication or Rich Site Summary, a system for publishing content that is changed or updated on a regular basis. For example, blog entries and online news reports have RSS feeds that include either full text or summaries of content.

RTW (real-time Web)   technology and techniques that allow people to receive information as soon as it is uploaded to the Web and to contribute content that is published as it is being uploaded.

satire   when a person or a text is imitated in order to poke fun or to ridicule, often politically motivated.

semantic matching   connecting information based on correspondences among ONTOLOGIES.

social media   Internet-based applications that allow people to create and exchange content and information.

social networking sites   web-based services that allow you to construct a public or semi-public profile within a bounded system, to connect and interact with other users with whom you share a connection or interests, and to view your list of connections and those made by others within the system.

statement of ethics concerning research on human participants   the policy of an academic institution that requires you to document your intended research activities if they involve human participants who could potentially be harmed by the techniques you will be using.

style   the way something is said or accomplished as opposed to the SUBSTANCE of the communication. Although tyle and substance are interrelated, style is more a matter of form than of content.

substance   the content of a communication or its message. See also STYLE.

syndication   web syndication ensures that a notice about updated content is sent to subscribers so that they are aware of changes to their favourite sites.

synthesis   the combination or fusion of parts or elements so as to form a whole.

tag   a keyword and a form of metadata assigned to an image, file, or some other piece of information online. Tags allow information to be found and retrieved in a search enabled by keyword-based classification.

theoretical framework   the component of the document that sets forth and makes explicit the system of principles that serve as the constructs that will be used to provide an account of the phenomena under investigation.

theory   a set of interconnected notions, ideas, rules, or principles that together describe, explain, or provide an account of some thing, situation, or phenomenon based on general laws or rules that exist independently of the thing under scrutiny.

thesis   at the most basic level, a thesis is a statement that introduces and summarizes the content of an essay by presenting the main argument, claims, ideas, or conclusion. On a larger level, a thesis is a term for a study that is longer and more complex than a term paper, but not as large and complex as a doctoral dissertation or a book.

trailer   a video advertisement that uses inventive editing and is intended to generate attention and create excitement about a project.

transdisciplinary research   research in which real life contexts—such as some actual problem or situation—guide investigations that extend beyond particular disciplinary boundaries.

video embedding a feature, such as that offered by YouTube, that allows you to insert video clips into your blog or website.

vlog a video blog; a form of blog that primarily uses video (e.g., web television).

VoIP (Voice over Internet Protocol) a technology that transmits your voice, image, and instant messages over the Internet instead of through the telephone network.

wiki a website that can be accessed and edited by a number of different people so that it facilitates collaborative work.

XML (Extensible Markup Language) a file format that defines the rules for encoding documents so they can be read by both people and computers. XML makes it possible for the information on the site to be published once and viewed by many different programs.

Index